Saved by
the Bellini

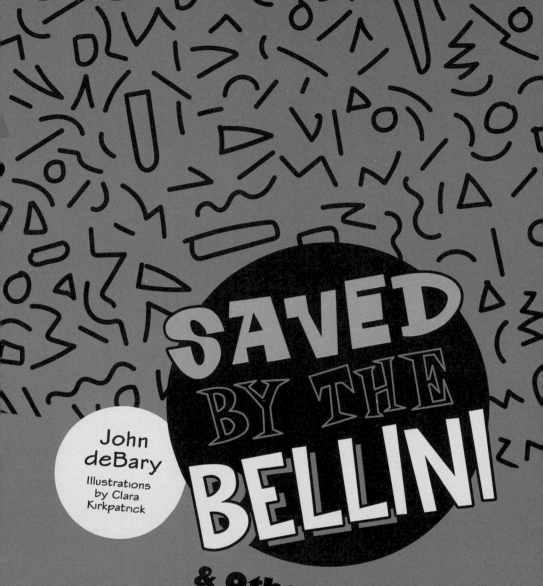

SAVED BY THE BELLINI

John deBary

Illustrations by Clara Kirkpatrick

BELLINI

& Other '90s-Inspired Cocktails

Foreword by Tiffani Thiessen

This book is dedicated to all the
people who wish they could go back
in time to change the song lyrics they
used in their senior yearbooks.

CONTENTS

AS SEEN ON . . .
TV, Movies & Books

DISCOVERY ZONE
Toys, Technology & Games

MALL MADNESS

Style & Fashion

SNACK PACK

Food & Drink

NOW THAT'S WHAT I CALL ...

Music

Foreword

Ahhhhhh, the '90s. Or, as I tell my kids, the glorious days of stone-washed denim, see-through phones that plugged directly into the wall, and the best compact music machine ever created: the Walkman.

Between the music, the movies, the fashion, and THE HAIR!, the '90s feel like they were a lifetime ago, and yet so much of what we love from then seems like it never went away. It was an iconic decade for a lot of reasons, and I love any chance to revisit it. The '90s have an extra-special place in my heart. I think it's because our generation is obsessed with nostalgia. I am, too—and that's why I'm so into this book!

I'm delighted that people like John deBary are paying such loving tribute to the '90s, even thirty years later. It is a joy to revisit this magical decade in the form of these clever, delicious (and hilarious!) cocktail recipes.

I love using food and drinks to connect: with friends, family—even with ourselves. I've loved cooking and entertaining ever since I was little. I always made feasts and baked during the holidays with my mom and all the women in my family. Years later I had the opportunity to take the leap into unscripted television. My show *Dinner at Tiffani's* was unlike anything I'd ever done before, but it showcased how I really love to spend my time—and heck, I got paid for it, too! I was honored to write my first cookbook, *Pull Up a Chair,*

to be able to share my love of cooking with even more people. The book has a whole chapter on no-sweat entertaining. Particularly when it comes to cocktails, I'm inspired by the classics, but I'm also constantly thinking of ways I can reinvent them for fun occasions.

So you can see how *Saved by the Bellini* is a unique blend of my interests!

This book is a brilliant walk down memory lane, from the shows and movies we were watching to the games we were playing to the clothes we were sporting and even to the snacks we were eating after school. If you didn't get your straw stuck in your CapriSun pouch, were you even a kid in the '90s? The idea of being able to share these memories with an entirely new set of people today is wild—and super fun!

The Saved by the Bellini drink is my favorite, for obvious reasons, but the Ultra-Cosmopolitan brings me to a certain time and place, too. I am tempted to batch up the Ay Mockarena mocktail to start educating my kids on all these awesome references! The amazingly creative cocktails throughout this book make it clear that John loves the '90s just as much as I do—and I bet you do, too. It's kind of crazy to think that we all grew up in different places and had different experiences in our childhoods, but these shared pop culture experiences bring us all together.

My best advice would be to keep your special moments in the ol' memory bank, because you'll never know when you'll want to cash them in later.

—*Tiffani Thiessen*

Introduction

I am a proud child of the 1990s. I was born in 1982, and I was old enough on December 31, 1989, that I remember watching the ball drop and hearing the TV host, a young female news anchor, or maybe a long-forgotten MTV VJ, giddy with manufactured excitement, announce that it was about time we "flushed the '80s down the toilet."

Explaining why everyone thought the 1980s was such a terrible decade is a topic for another book, but I suppose one reason for everyone's excitement was the widespread idea that the future would be better than the past. This notion made intuitive sense to all of us. When the clock struck midnight on January 1, 1990, we were looking forward to so many things we didn't even know about yet: the information superhighway, Nintendo 64, the dissolution of the Soviet Union, *Final Fantasy VII*, Crystal Pepsi, designer babies, *The Matrix*, and one of the most prolonged periods of economic expansion in our nation's history. Also, three *Star Trek* TV spinoffs, the de-pathologizing of homosexuality, and the Tamagotchi.

It was an eventful ten years.

But as the decade progressed, a sense of dread took over, and the years began to feel like they would be the last on Earth. Of course, the bellwether was Prince's apocalyptic "Party Like It's 1999" smash hit, but increasing climate change (thanks for bringing that to our attention, Al Gore) and the forecasted Y2K computer glitch that would bring accidental nuclear annihilation loomed large over our collective psyches, increasingly so with each passing year. There was a shared sense that we had to get it all out before the clock struck midnight on December 31, 1999, when everything would come crashing down. Of course, everything did come crashing down, but not until September 11, 2001, a date that ushered in an era of endless wars and xenophobic nationalism that gave rise to emboldened right-wing political populism. Now, amid a global climate crisis, war, the collapse of objectivity, a rollback of civil rights, and a seemingly never-ending global pandemic, an extremely valid case can be made for the '90s being the last good decade our generation will ever see.

But enough gloom and doom.

The '90s gave us so much to celebrate—and what better way to do just that than to make a bunch of cocktails? The drink recipes contained in this book are modern, up-to-date recipes made in loving homage to some of the best things that happened during the iconic decade.

Aside from being alive and aware during this decade, I have some other relevant qualifications for writing such a book. I started bartending professionally at the award-winning neo-speakeasy PDT in 2008. Actually, even before that, I took a bartending course in college—but it was mostly an excuse to drink every Thursday night; I learned next to nothing there. After five and a half years behind the bar at PDT, I spent nine years working for David Chang and the Momofuku restaurant group, first as a bartender and then as the company's bar director. I opened nearly ten restaurants, trained dozens of bartenders, and developed countless cocktails and menus.

In 2020 I published my first book, *Drink What You Want: The Subjective Guide to Making Objectively Delicious Drinks*. In it, I go into a lot of detail about the philosophical underpinnings of cocktails, learning what you like about them, and how you can create them intuitively to suit your tastes. I assume this might be the first cocktail book you've ever read, so you'll get all the important basics here, but I encourage you to continue your drinking journey with *DWYW* after having a blast with this one.

Now tie that flannel around your waist, throw your pony through a Topsy Tail, and prepare for a totally fly tour through The Best Decade Ever. Our first stop is TV, movies, and books; then we'll take a ride in our Geo Tracker to the land of toys, tech, and games; afterward, we'll Skip-It over to the land of iconic fashion trends; and before we pop in a cassette to chaotically record Ace of Base songs off the radio, we'll open up a can of whoop-ass on some bitchin' '90s food and drinks.

And if you don't think this sounds like a sweet-ass time, well, then, that's like, your opinion, man . . .

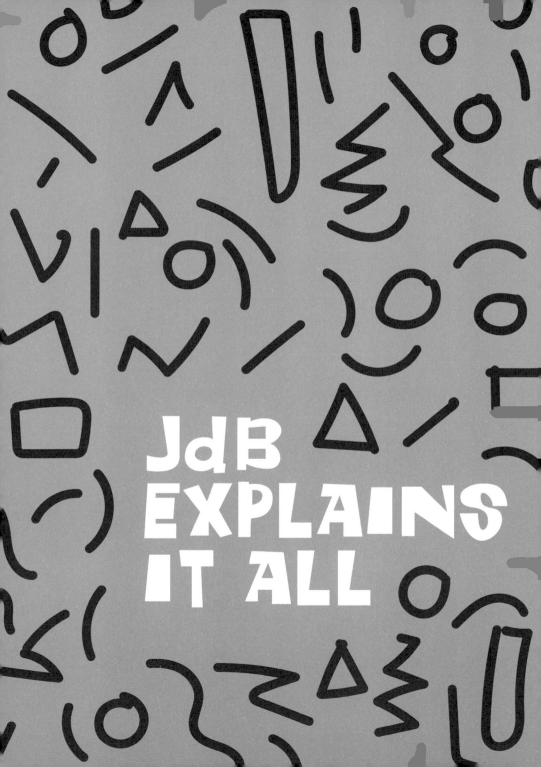

cocktail basics

Ingredients

Absinthe Steeped in myth and mystery, absinthe is a high-proof spirit made—similarly to gin—by infusing neutral spirits with botanicals: wormwood, anise, fennel, hyssop, and others. There is no truth to the myth that absinthe will cause hallucinations; it's just a strong sprit with a distinctive aroma that, when wielded judiciously, adds amazing depth to cocktails.

Aquavit This clear spirit is the Scandinavian cousin of gin. It is predominantly flavored with caraway and star anise and is sometimes aged in barrels. Some might call this an acquired taste;

I personally love it and find it works in surprising ways.

Bourbon The quintessential American whiskey is made predominantly from corn with rye, wheat, and other grains. It's aged for at least two years in new, charred-oak containers and is extremely versatile in cocktails. It imparts a roast-y, vanilla-inflected sweetness.

Cognac This is a French grape brandy that's been aged in oak.

Gin This versatile spirit is, in a way, flavored vodka. Gin producers take a neutral base spirit and infuse it with botanicals such as juniper, cardamom, licorice, and citrus, just to name a few. Gin is made in a huge variety of styles, so it's hard to generalize, but most is bright and pine-y. Any gin that has on its label the words *London Dry*—referring to the less-sweet styles of gin that are widely popular—should work well for the drinks in this book.

Irish Whiskey A globally popular spirit made in Ireland from malted barley. It's aged in oak barrels and is a mellow, malty presence in cocktails.

Kirschwasser The name is German for "cherry water"; it's an unaged spirit made from, you guessed it, cherries.

Mezcal This broad category comprises tequila as well as other Mexican agave–based spirits. Also made from agave but generally unaged, this spirit is smoky and vegetal.

Pisco This unaged grape spirit is produced in Peru and Chile. Peruvian pisco is more commonly available in the United States, so that's what I'm familiar with. Pisco is produced in such a way that the grapey goodness of the raw

ingredients shines through; it's a great choice for lively, refreshing cocktails.

Rum This spirit category is one of the broadest and most diverse. All rum is made from some form of sugar (usually molasses), and some but not all are aged in oak. Overproof rums can be 50 to 60% alcohol by volume (ABV) and above. Goslings is a specific brand of rum made in Bermuda with a distinctive, rich molasses character.

Rye Whiskey Another classically American spirit that's made from, yes, rye grain. Rye recipes also contain corn, wheat, and other grains, and, like bourbon, are aged in charred oak containers. Also very versatile in drinks, rye stands a bit hotter and grassier next to bourbon.

Scotch Whisky Like Irish whiskey, Scotch is made from barley. In the case of Scotch, though, many producers impart their whisky with smoke from burnt peat—which is literally fossilized swamp matter— to create an intensely smoky and medicinal spirit. Scotch styles vary widely between producers and regions; if you're looking for a middle-of-the-road pick, go with a bottle that has the word *blended* on the label as opposed to the more idiosyncratic single malts.

Soju Believe it or not, soju is the world's most consumed spirit. It's made in Korea primarily from sweet potatoes. Not to be confused with Japanese shochu, which is similar to soju but is usually made in a number of different styles, soju tends to be more neutral.

Tequila This versatile spirit is made in the southwestern Mexican state of Jalisco from agave plants. These fibrous plants are grown, cooked, and fermented to create a vegetal, refreshing spirit. Reposado tequilas are aged up to three months in oak barrels, while blanco tequilas are aged less than two months, if at all. The most important thing to understand when buying tequila is to make sure it says *100% de Agave* on the label—that's how you know it's the good stuff.

Vodka This is the most neutral of the spirits. It's usually made from grain or potatoes but retains very little of the flavor of the raw ingredients. What it lacks in flavor it makes up for in versatility—you can successfully apply vodka in a wide

array of situations. Flavored vodkas, like citron vodka, also have a time and a place.

Allspice Liqueur Sometimes called "pimento dram," this piquant liqueur is available from a few different producers. It's made by infusing allspice berries into rum.

Amaretto An Italian liqueur made from apricot kernels infused into brandy.

Bénédictine A French herbal liqueur made from a proprietary blend of twenty-seven botanicals, including saffron, cinnamon, clove, and honey.

Campari This bright-red bitter Italian liqueur shows up across many classic cocktails. Its bittersweet, citrusy flavor comes from a closely guarded secret blend of botanicals.

Chambord Showing up in an unmistakable spherical and gold-adorned bottle, this French black raspberry liqueur is often overlooked but is a worthy addition to your home bar for its distinct berry flavor.

JdB Explains It All

Chartreuse Made by monks in a French monastery according to an ultra-secret recipe. The two main variants are yellow, which is lighter and has more chamomile and honey notes, and green, which is more bitter and medicinal with a slightly higher alcohol content. They're not interchangeable in drinks, so you will want to have a bottle of each handy.

Cherry Heering This is a somewhat hard-to-find Danish black cherry liqueur that is well worth the search thanks to its great balance of sweetness and acidity. Try ordering it online if your local liquor store doesn't stock it.

Crème de Cacao This liqueur is made from cocoa beans and in some cases additional flavorings. Brands don't vary hugely, but I always prefer the clear stuff versus the chocolate-brown version, as it gives you more control over the look of your drink.

Crème de Cassis This is an iconic French black currant liqueur. Although crème de cassis can be legally made anywhere, the specific variety crème de cassis de Dijon is made from a recipe that yields a slightly higher quality than the rest— you should seek it out.

Crème de Menthe A liqueur generally made from peppermint; like crème de cacao, you can find a colorless variety, which I prefer to the green-tinted version.

Kahlúa A Mexican coffee liqueur made from coffee, rum, vanilla, and caramel.

Midori Often derided as an unserious cocktail ingredient, Midori is a Japanese muskmelon liqueur made by Suntory. It has a vibrant green hue and unmistakable melon flavor. Nothing else is quite like it.

St-Germain An extremely popular French elderflower liqueur. Other elderflower liqueurs will work just fine as a substitute, but this brand is the gold standard.

Orange Liqueur Three you'll need to know here: **Grand Marnier, Cointreau,** and **blue curaçao.** Grand Marnier and Cointreau are both French, with Grand Marnier being a bit richer and more vanilla-inflected than Cointreau, which is relatively brighter and more bitter. Blue curaçao is more straightforwardly flavored, with a delightful addition of blue coloring. Some may call this characteristic tacky, but sometimes drinking a blue drink is just fun.

Other Liqueurs You'll find a grab bag here: **raspberry, strawberry, banana,** and **rose.** They are all pretty self-explanatory, and while the gap between the cheap and the expensive stuff is not wide, like most things in life, you get what you pay for.

Madeira A fortified wine made on the Portuguese island of the same name. Its production process uses heat and time to oxidize the wine, so there's no need to store it in the refrigerator after opening. For cocktails, a medium-dry style works best.

Port A fortified wine from Portugal that is generally sweeter than sherry. Tawny port is a medium-sweet, nutty variety.

Sherry A fortified wine made in the Jerez region of Spain. Sherries can range from super dry and acidic to almost liqueur-like in sweetness. The drinks in this book use Fino, the driest style. Consume it immediately or refrigerate after opening.

Vermouth These are fortified and aromatized wines—in other words, wines that have extra alcohol and flavorings added to them. Dry vermouth is generally associated with France and is light and vegetal, whereas sweet vermouth is more of an Italian product and is sweeter with richer flavorings. Both are made from a base of white wine and should either be consumed upon opening or stored in the refrigerator so the flavors don't degrade.

Angostura Bitters Super concentrated cocktail flavoring made from bitter botanicals like gentian according to a secret recipe. When a cocktail calls for bitters, this product is usually what is meant.

Orange Bitters A concentrated cocktail flavoring that has predominant notes of orange, although some producers use other flavorings for a more complex profile. I prefer Bitter Truth or Angostura's offerings.

Lemons and Limes The two key citrus fruits you'll need for this book. Lemon juice is a bit rounder in flavor than lime juice, but in both cases you should use the freshest juice possible; after twenty-four hours they start to lose their vibrancy.

Oranges and Grapefruits These two fruits (and their juices) are used less frequently than lemon or lime but can play important roles nonetheless. Their juices are more challenging to work with in drinks because they're less concentrated, but where they shine is their peels: both fruits contain lovely aromatic oils in their skins.

Watermelon Juice This is a fun ingredient, but it must always be juiced fresh because it tastes stale quickly after juicing. If you don't have a fancy juicer (I don't!), just toss chunks in the blender and use a fine-mesh strainer to separate out the solids.

Filtered Water Any flat water you use in a cocktail should be filtered in order to remove any chlorine or other impurities or additives that would contribute to any "off" taste.

Ice Obviously, ice is a critical ingredient in drinks. You'll need ice to make drinks, when stirring and shaking them, and when serving drinks. Buying large ice molds to make big cubes for on-the-rocks drinks is always fun but never a requirement.

Sparkling Water These two words together can mean anything from homemade seltzer to sparkling mineral water. Homemade sparkling waters tend to have rough bubbles; store-bought seltzers have medium bubbles; and sparkling mineral waters have finer bubbles and a bit more mineral texture. I like to use store-bought seltzer in cocktails (Vintage is my brand of choice), but feel free to use your personal favorite.

Cold Brew Coffee Concentrate My preferred way to incorporate coffee into drinks. Heat-based methods of making coffee create a more perishable brew that might last a day or two in the refrigerator, but cold brew should last at least a week. Make it yourself or buy it.

Ginger Ale Don't confuse this with ginger beer, which is a more intense and peppery expression of ginger that would overpower the recipes in this book. Any ginger ale you find in a supermarket will work well here. We'll occasionally use a super-concentrated ginger syrup (page 54) to dial it up.

Ice Ice Baby Don't forget to use filtered water when you're making ice, too.

Honey This is an ingredient that needs to be mixed with water in order to incorporate well into cocktails. The variety of honey you get is not super important, but I would avoid more intense honeys like manuka in favor of the milder orange blossom or clover.

Tonic Water This bittersweet soda runs the gamut from syrupy, mass-market stuff to lighter and more refined artisanal varieties. The drinks in this book will work fine with whatever you pick.

Ginger Candy Slices of ginger that have been soaked in sugar, these spicy, chewy treats are a great way to garnish any ginger-based drink. You can find them online, and they last basically forever in a cool, dry place, ready for whenever the mood strikes.

Luxardo Cherries Ah, the definitive cocktail cherry. They're made by an Italian spirits producer and they are one-of-a-kind delicious. Luxardos are a little on the pricey side but well worth the expense, both for the cherries themselves and the decadent syrup they're packed in.

Tapioca Pearls Also known as boba, these are used extensively in Asian sweet teas. Basically flavorless, they offer a delightful chewy texture to drinks. They are easy to prepare and find online.

(Don't) Say My Name A Note on Brands

The recipes in this book are designed to work with a wide variety of brands within any given category, and I only call for brands in ingredient lists when absolutely essential to the outcome of the recipe. In other words, if a recipe calls for vodka, there's a good chance it will work with whatever your favorite is. But if the recipe calls for, say, Campari, the drink is designed to work with that specific brand of liqueur only, and a substitution is not advised.

Tools

Shaking Set Sometimes called a Boston shaker, this is a two-piece set with a small and large tin. As the name might suggest, you use it to shake cocktails, and you can also use one half of it (usually the small one) to stir drinks. If you do have a dedicated mixing glass for stirring drinks, by all means, please use it.

Jiggers Find one that measures half an ounce and three-quarters of an ounce and another that measures one ounce and two ounces. A fun, handy fact that will give you a surprising amount of mileage: a tablespoon is half an ounce, and a quarter cup is two ounces.

Strainer Sometimes referred to as a Hawthorne strainer. The key here is the spring that gives you a snug fit around the inside of your shaking tin and can strain out ice chunks.

Barspoon To stir drinks, you need something long and slender. There are spoons made just for this purpose, or you can use a chopstick or something like that.

Juicer However you get the job done of extracting citrus juice from the fruit is acceptable, whether it's with a fork, a reamer, an "elbow" juicer, or something electric. Juicing is hard work, so know that tools exist to make it easier, and find the one that works best for you.

Who Will Stray-ee-ain Your Soul? While we're on the topic of citrus juice, be sure to always, always strain pulp and seeds from your juice before using it.

Fine-Mesh Strainer This is a sieve, basically. Large ones will work when straining significant quantities of liquid, and small ones are preferable when straining individual drinks. I cannot recommend a gold coffee filter highly enough; they are reusable, and their fine mesh will help give your drinks great clarity and texture.

Muddler You can buy dedicated cocktail muddlers made out of wood or food-grade silicone, or you can use a rolling pin or an otherwise blunt, long object to mash up solid ingredients into your drinks.

Microplane Sometimes referred to as a "rasp," this tool helps you create shavings of citrus rind, nutmeg, cinnamon, and the like.

Peelers Typically used for things like carrots and potatoes in cooking, peelers are also key for citrus when making drinks.

Knife It's worth the money to invest in at least one high-quality knife. A good choice is an 8-inch chef's knife, or get a small paring knife if you want to save space.

Ice Cube Trays Even if you have an ice maker, trays are great for when you want to freeze other stuff besides plain water. Plus, there are molds for two-inch cubes that are nice for drinks served on the rocks.

Blender One of the most useful appliances a home bartender can purchase. They're essential for blended ice drinks, of course, but also come in handy when making syrups and infusions.

Food Processor This tool has similar functionality to a blender, but its long blades and flatter form factor help to process solid items like ginger and pineapple into pulpy mashes for drinks.

Giving Him Something He Can Peel I prefer a basic Y-peeler; the blade usually dulls after a while, so I recommend buying a pack of cheap ones and replacing them when the time comes—six months to a year.

Picks Cocktail picks are used when you want to perch a garnish on the rim of a glass, like a cherry or piece of candy. Wooden toothpicks are a fine option, but if you want to class things up a bit, go for elegant metal picks, which have the bonus of being reusable.

Ice Cream Machine Making drinks-adjacent desserts is a true joy. If you are so inclined, you can find ice cream machines with their own cooling units, but you can also find inexpensive (and smaller) options that rely on chilling a bucket in the freezer, and they work great, too.

Straws Drinking with a straw is a completely different experience than drinking directly from a glass. They help to bring liquid up from the bottom and act as a sort of filter against ice or anything else solid-ish in the glass. Metal or glass straws are great for home use. Wider bubble tea straws are, of course, essential for bubble tea, but they are also superior for slushies and other frozen drinks.

Glassware The drinks in this book call for the following styles: cocktail coupe, old fashioned glass, tall (or highball) glass, wine glass, heatproof mug, and tropical-style mug. But honestly, sometimes the best glass is just the one available to you.

Semi-Chilled Kind of Life Any cold drink will be improved by pouring into a pre-chilled glass. Plan ahead by placing your glasses in the freezer at least 30 minutes prior to making your drinks. But if you forget about it, you can also fill the glass with ice and then dump the ice before serving. Or, if you don't feel like it, your drinks will be just fine in room-temperature glasses.

This Is How We Do It

the 411
on making
the most
excellent
drinks

Measuring

After you've done your planning, shopping, and prep, the first step for making any drink is to measure. In general, you will use jiggers, the dedicated tool for cocktail measuring, to pour out the correct amounts of each ingredient for your drinks. When you measure into a jigger, you must fill it all the way, until it's just dribbling over, to ensure an accurate measurement every time. Free-pouring, or not measuring, is a valid way to make drinks, but the trade-off is that you won't get the precise measurements that many drinks require in order to taste just right. Of course, once you have the hang of making drinks and a confident sense of your own preferences, feel free to play around by adjusting measurements slightly—but be sure you really nail the basics before freestyling.

Once you've assembled your ingredients, you need to integrate, chill, dilute, and, in some cases, aerate them to "finish" the cocktail. So when do you shake and when do you stir?

Shaking

You want to shake drinks that contain citrus, dairy, and eggs because these ingredients contain solids that need more work to fully integrate into your cocktail. Once you've poured your ingredients into the small shaking tin, fill with ice, close, and shake the living hell out of it for about 15 seconds. There's some nuance to shaking that we don't need to worry about here, but the key is to shake long and hard so that the ingredients mix and are chilled and diluted by the ice. The action should whip the ingredients into a nice froth.

Some novice bartenders have trouble opening the shaker after they're done shaking. This happens because the ice has chilled the air inside the shaker, causing it to contract and create a vacuum. Whoa, science is wild! Break the seal by popping the shaking set against the palm of your hand, or just use brute strength to pull them apart.

Stirring

Stirring is the preferred method when you're only dealing with translucent ingredients that need less coaxing to mix fully. You can use the small tin of a shaking set to stir your drinks, but a pint glass or other dedicated mixing vessel will work just fine. Stirring is a gentler process than shaking; the drink is still mixed, but the dilution and chilling are less pronounced, and it shouldn't result in any bubbles or frothiness.

Straining

Whether shaking or stirring, in most cases, you'll then want to separate the drink from the ice. You accomplish this using a strainer (sometimes called a Hawthorne strainer). This device fits over the end of the shaker and has a spring to help filter out big ice chunks.

Garnishing

Although they may seem frivolous, cocktail garnishes are anything but. In addition to adding a bit of visual flair, some garnishes, like citrus peels, provide an additional aromatic layer on top thanks to the essential oils found in citrus skin. That layer can be an important part of the drink experience. When garnishing with citrus, use a vegetable peeler to create a two- to three-inch swath, then pinch the peel over the surface of the drink to express the oils, and finish by placing the peel on the edge of the glass. (You can also cut a slit in the peel to perch it snugly on the rim, or if you want to be minimalist, toss the peel once you've expressed the oils.) Other garnishes, like cherries and ginger candy, can be stuck with a pick and arranged on the rim of the glass.

tv,
movies
&
books

AS
SEEN
ON . . .

Heart of the Ocean

The movie *Titanic* was inescapable—and so it was no surprise when it became the first movie ever to hit the billion-dollar revenue mark. The story centers around socialite Rose DeWitt Bukater, who was given a massive fifty-six-carat blue diamond necklace, the Heart of the Ocean, by her pompous and doomed fiancé. She falls in love with the penniless artist from steerage, Jack (played by Leo DiCaprio), but in a classic Rich Person move, hoards the driftwood that could have saved them both, condemning him to a freezing-cold watery grave. (Leo's hair in the sad scene gave new meaning to the then-popular style "frosted tips.") The necklace is assumed lost at sea, but (spoiler alert) Rose kept it, only to secretly toss it overboard while on another ship decades later.

Let's just say the movie was full of a lot of bad nautical choices—as opposed to this drink, which is a great choice. Dark rum usually spends a few years in watertight oak barrels, while Madeira is a fortified wine from the island of Madeira, which is smack in the middle of the North Atlantic Ocean. Drink one of these and try not to think about what you would have done with a million-dollar necklace . . . besides throw it overboard.

1½ ounces dark rum
1½ ounces medium-dry Madeira
½ ounce rose liqueur

 In a mixing glass or small shaking tin, combine all the ingredients. Add ice and stir gently for 20 seconds. Strain into a cocktail coupe.

As Seen On . . .

Absinthe-Crag

We really can't talk about '90s TV without talking about Nickelodeon—it had something for everyone, from its youngest *Blue's Clues* fans (Nick Jr.) to the old-timey rerun set (Nick at Nite) and the rest of us in between. The network killed at cartoons in a way that was fresh, and it also excelled at action competitions, including *Double Dare*, *Legends of the Hidden Temple*, and my personal favorite: *GUTS*. This physical runaround culminated in the scaling of the neon-lit Aggro Crag in the hopes of bringing home a piece of it—a jagged, glowing green trophy.

Through the magic of TV, the obstacle-laden mountain (the scaling of which required a helmet as well as both knee and elbow pads) felt somehow huge despite being built entirely indoors. It was an absurd mash-up—and so, too, is this drink. Yoo-hoo is the chocolate milk–adjacent beverage that somehow managed to have an air of nutritiousness despite being anything but, and absinthe is a high-proof botanical spirit that originated in Switzerland. We'll top it off with a bit of trivia: from 1989 to 2000 (aka the '90s), Yoo-hoo was owned by Pernod Ricard, one of the world's biggest producers of absinthe. This pairing might sound unlikely at first, but like this iconic game show, it's a challenge worth accepting.

4 ounces Yoo-hoo
1½ ounces absinthe

 In a shaker, combine all the ingredients. Add ice and shake vigorously for 15 seconds. Strain into a cocktail coupe.

McCallister Wassail

I was a pretty independent kid, so the idea of being accidentally left behind by my family for a few days, the way Kevin McCallister was in *Home Alone*, actually sounded kinda nice. I was also big on forts and swings and other elaborate house modifications in the name of fun, so *Home Alone* was one of my comfort movies growing up. (I was also envious of Macaulay Culkin for getting to be an actor in a cool movie instead of going to boring school like I had to.)

A wassail is a spiced, large-format drink that's typically served during the holidays in cold-weather regions, such as 671 Lincoln Avenue in Winnetka, the Chicago suburb where Kevin made his mark. Think of it as a lighter aperitif to the heavier, more after-dinner-y eggnog. Since we're just kids here, this recipe is alcohol-free (except for the bitters, which add a negligible amount—about as much as aftershave). But if you want a little something extra for the grown-ups, try bourbon, Cognac, or dark rum, an ounce and a half per cup and a half of wassail, added at the end.

15 to 20 whole cloves

1 vanilla bean, seeds scraped, or 2 teaspoons pure vanilla extract (see Note)

20 cardamom pods

12 star anise pods

Peels of 3 medium oranges

4 cups apple cider

25 dashes Angostura bitters

In a large pan over medium heat, combine the cloves, vanilla bean and scraped seeds, cardamom, and star anise. Cook, stirring constantly, until fragrant, about 3 minutes. Add the orange peels, cider, and bitters. Stir occasionally, until warmed through (do not boil), about 10 minutes. Ladle into heatproof mugs.

Note: If you are using vanilla extract instead of the bean, add the liquid with the cider and bitters.

As Seen On . . .

Life Finds a Whey

Even though I was eleven years old when *Jurassic Park* hit theaters in 1993, I saw it at least three times opening week and instinctively knew I was witnessing one of the most significant events in cinematic history. One of the iconic lines from the movie is from Jeff Goldblum's character commenting on the inevitability of calamity: "Life finds a way." This line is particularly poignant once the imperiled cast discovers that the dinosaurs are able to switch genders and reproduce.

When it comes to making drinks, we can get almost as resourceful as those gender-switching dinos by using often-overlooked ingredients in novel ways. Whey is the byproduct of making cheese—when milk is dosed with an acidic element, a coagulation of protein molecules is triggered. Using whey in a cocktail lends a mild creamy note while allowing other ingredients to take more of a starring role. You can use a plant-based milk if you prefer, but I, for one, would never pass up an opportunity to play scientist in my kitchen.

8 ounces Isla Nublar Whey (recipe
  follows)
2 ounces white rum

2 ounces crème de cacao
1 cup fresh mango, chopped

In a blender, combine all the ingredients. Add 4 cups of ice. Blend on medium speed until smooth, 15 to 20 seconds. Divide the drink between two old fashioned glasses and serve with bubble tea straws.

Isla Nublar Whey

Makes about 1 cup whey plus 1 cup fresh ricotta

2 cups whole milk
2 ounces fresh lemon juice

In a medium bowl, stir together the milk and lemon juice. Let sit, uncovered, at room temperature until curds begin to form, about 30 minutes. Strain the mixture through a fine-mesh strainer into an airtight container, reserving the ricotta-like solids, if desired. Store the whey and the ricotta in airtight containers in the refrigerator for up to 1 week.

Sanderson Sister Sour

The 1993 camp classic *Hocus Pocus* featured Bette Midler, Sarah Jessica Parker, and Kathy Najimy as the villainous Sanderson sisters hanged for practicing witchcraft, only to be accidentally brought back to life (and then un-brought back to life) by unsuspecting '90s kids (hi, Thora Birch!). The sisters are obsessed with eternal youth and use various tricks and potions to try to suck the life force out of the town's children.

A bartender's job is not unlike that of a witch. Both consult ancient texts and obtain obscure ingredients to concoct mind- and body-altering substances. The key distinction is that bartenders almost always want to make people feel *good*. Enter this sour: the drink features floral, fruity liqueurs along with pisco, a refreshing Peruvian grape brandy. It won't turn you into an immortal talking cat, but it will definitely make you feel young and fun.

¾ ounce crème de cassis
¾ ounce St-Germain
¾ ounce fresh lime juice
½ ounce pisco
½ ounce Turbo Honey Syrup (page 63)
OPTIONAL GARNISH: EDIBLE GLITTER

 In a shaker, combine the drink ingredients. Fill with ice and shake vigorously for 15 seconds. Strain into a cocktail coupe. Stir in edible glitter, if the mood possesses you.

The Costanzas' Marble Rye

Definitively, the best television show of the '90s was *Seinfeld*. To this day, most of the humor holds up—even though these days, about 80 percent of the situations the characters found themselves in could have been fixed with a cell phone. This group of aimless adults living in Manhattan of course loved food; Monk's, their diner, was practically a main character. To me, the show's funniest food plotline was the marble rye incident, in which George's pathologically cheap and petty parents rescind from the parents of Susan, their soon-to-be daughter-in-law, a gift of marble rye bread when it goes unacknowledged. The hilarity that ensues can't be done justice in words, but the fact is that marble rye is one of the world's best breads.

The marble coloring of the bread is usually achieved with cocoa powder, and the bread is flavored with caraway seeds. This combination seamlessly transitions to liquid form by infusing rye whiskey with cocoa nibs and caraway seeds to construct an otherwise straightforward Manhattan. Sip it while you revisit other iconic funny moments such as the Fusilli Jerry, No Soup for You, the Butter Shave, and how Elaine got Jerry and George's sitcom cancelled by sneezing on a pasta primavera.

2 ounces Caraway-Cacao Rye
   Whiskey (recipe follows)
1 ounce sweet vermouth

2 dashes Angostura bitters
1 dash orange bitters

 In a mixing glass or shaking tin, combine all the ingredients. Add ice and stir gently for 20 seconds. Strain into a cocktail coupe.

Caraway-Cacao Rye Whiskey
Makes about 12 ounces

12 ounces rye whiskey
2 tablespoons cacao nibs
2 tablespoons caraway seeds

In an airtight container, combine the rye, cacao nibs, and caraway seeds

and stir briefly. Cover and let sit at room temperature overnight or at least 8 hours. Strain through a fine-mesh strainer into an airtight container. Store in a cool, dry place for up to 6 months.

Guinan Tonic

Star Trek: The Next Generation gave us one of the best fictional bartenders ever: Guinan, played by Whoopi Goldberg. Legend has it that Whoopi was so inspired by Nichelle Nichols, who played Uhura on the original *Star Trek* series, that she lobbied the show's creator, Gene Roddenberry, for a part-time role on the spinoff. Guinan was solicitous, pseudo-immortal, and always "working on something," meaning she was frequently surrounded by bottles and potions, concocting elaborate drinks. Basically, she was a nerdy mixologist decades before a handful of East Village bros thought it was cool. Guinan exemplifies hospitality, thanks to her ability to listen and her constant desire to expose her guests to new things.

In one episode, she served Worf, the grumpy Klingon security officer, a glass of prune juice, and he loved it. "A warrior's drink!" he exclaimed. While Worf only drank straight prune juice, I have to imagine that Guinan played around with it in other ways. I paired the stewed sweetness of the juice with a middle-of-the-road red wine that, along with the bitterness and acidity from the tonic water, creates a moody yet low-alcohol sipper to help you unwind after a long day defending the Federation.

4 ounces light red wine, such as pinot noir
3 ounces prune juice
3 dashes Angostura bitters
1½ ounces tonic water

 In a mixing glass or shaking tin, combine the wine, prune juice, and bitters. Add ice and stir gently for 20 seconds. Strain into a wine glass and top with the tonic water.

As Seen On . . .

~~Virgin~~ Who Can't Drive

makes
1 drink

It is not unreasonable to divide human history into two eras: before Amy Heckerling's 1995 film *Clueless*, and, well, after. The film produced so many cultural treasures—from the yellow plaid skirt set all the way to "As if!"—that it's hard to imagine a world in which we do not have this gem. If somehow you are unfamiliar, the story centers on rich Beverly Hills high schooler Cher Horowitz (played to perfection by Alicia Silverstone), who tries to improve the social standing of newcomer Tai Frasier (RIP Brittany Murphy). In a pivotal, climactic scene toward the end of the film, Tai delivers to Cher this eternally unforgettable, searing-hot burn: "Why am I even listening to you? You're a virgin who can't drive." If you tell me you've never tried to insult someone with these words, you're probably a liar.

While Cher might have been a virgin, the occasion of her getting together with Josh (Paul Rudd, swoon) is reason enough for a drink these frisky teens might have concocted themselves. Despite the fact that Cher tells Mr. Hall she does *not* drink coffee in order to avoid the growth-stunting effects of caffeine, she appears drinking it in at least two scenes, mentions something called a "mochachino," and *also* rolls with a can of Diet Coke at lunchtime. If Travis was going to spill a drink on Cher's Alaïa, she might have preferred this to whatever was in that party-in-the-Valley red plastic cup.

¾ ounce white rum
¾ ounce crème de cacao
½ ounce cold brew coffee concentrate
1 dash orange bitters
1½ ounces Diet Coke
GARNISH: LEMON PEEL

In a mixing glass or shaking tin, combine the rum, crème de cacao, cold brew, and orange bitters. Add ice and stir gently for 20 seconds. Strain into a cocktail coupe. Top with the Diet Coke. Garnish with a lemon peel expressed and placed on the rim of the glass.

This Is Your Brain on Drugs

From the mid-2020s, it feels safe to say that the dubious War on Drugs was an epic failure—drugs definitely won. Throughout the '90s, every other commercial on TV seemed to be a PSA against something: drugs, bullying, or inappropriate touching. The 1997 "this is your brain on drugs" spot is the most memorable of them all, using a fried egg to demonstrate the damage that drugs can do to your brain. Rachael Leigh Cook (who, to her credit, went on to be known for other dramatic roles, too) trashes her own kitchen and ends with the line: "Any questions?"

It's easy to forget that alcohol is a drug just like any other, and responsible usage of drugs is a key element of an enlightened society. The PSA was goofy then, and it's goofy now; it mostly has the effect of making me want to eat eggs (. . . and do drugs). Eggs are a great cocktail ingredient because they provide an airy matrix to support other elements. Here, the egg white lightens the intense flavors of caraway and cacao-infused rye, and even serves as a base for a few drops of THC tincture so you can celebrate drugs winning the war.

2 ounces Caraway-Cacao Rye Whiskey (page 46) or regular rye whiskey
¾ ounce Heart in a Blender Simple Syrup (page 141)
½ ounce fresh lemon juice
½ ounce fresh lime juice
¼ ounce absinthe
1 egg white
GARNISH: THC TINCTURE

 In a shaker, combine the drink ingredients and shake, without ice, for 5 seconds to whip up the egg white. Add ice to shaker and shake again vigorously for 15 seconds. Strain into a cocktail coupe. Dot the surface of the drink with the THC tincture. This is your brain on drinks.

As Seen On . . .

The Carlton

We all know about West Philadelphia–born-and-raised Will Smith, who was sent to Los Angeles to live with his uber-rich uncle—that's how he became *The Fresh Prince of Bel-Air*. But Will's cousin Carlton Banks came away from the show as an icon, inspiring and making famous an entire dance routine. Carlton was a lovable loser whose innocence and dorkiness were constant sources of comedic relief.

This milk cocktail (I said what I said) represents the state beverage of Pennsylvania but also pays homage to Carlton's innocence. It's a little naïve and perhaps not everyone's idea of a good time, but it's endearing nonetheless. If you want to act your age, try adding a bit of dark rum or Irish whiskey.

3 ounces whole milk or dairy-free milk
1 ounce Ultragrenadine (page 71)
1 ounce Ginger Syrup (recipe follows)
GARNISHES: LUXARDO CHERRY AND GINGER CANDY

 In a shaker, combine the drink ingredients. Add ice and shake vigorously for 15 seconds. Strain into a tall glass filled with ice. Garnish with a Luxardo cherry and ginger candy on a pick.

Ginger Syrup
Makes about 2½ cups

1 pound fresh unpeeled ginger,
   scrubbed and soaked in warm
   water for five minutes
2 cups granulated sugar

Using a juicer, juice the ginger according to the manufacturer's instructions. Alternatively, roughly chop the ginger and, in a blender or food processor, pulverize the ginger on high speed, about 45 seconds, then pour the liquid through a fine-mesh strainer, discarding the solids. Using either method, you should have approximately 1 cup ginger juice.

In a medium saucepan over medium heat, combine the ginger juice and sugar. Cook, stirring occasionally, until lightly boiling, then cook until all the sugar is dissolved, about 10 minutes. Remove the pan from the heat and allow the syrup to cool for at least 30 minutes before using. Store in an airtight container in the refrigerator for up to 1 month or in the freezer for up to 4 months.

The Juicer

I loved, and still love, watching infomercials. When they weren't straight-up homoerotic (hi, Bowflex) they usually offered the promise of wonders in the kitchen, which made my young heart go pitter-patter. Jack LaLanne was a body builder and fitness mogul who created fitness clubs, wrote books, and hawked juicers on Saturday morning TV. One Christmas, I launched a begging campaign for a Jack LaLanne juicer, and it bore fruit. Unfortunately, the juicer broke after just three months, cutting short my amateur vegetable mixology career. And we've since realized that a lot of the "good" stuff is removed from fruits and veggies when they go through such machines (see: fiber).

As the professional drinks-slinger that I am now, I don't even have a juicer in my kitchen. Instead, I use a blender to create this low-ABV reimagination of a "healthy" juice smoothie that leaves intact alllll the chunky, health-promoting fibrous bits. While there is very little to call health-promoting when it comes to alcohol, both gin and Chartreuse started out as health tonics before becoming strictly recreational. I'd never describe an alcoholic beverage as good for you, but this one might be the closest I'll ever get. If you ditch the gin and Chartreuse, you're pretty close.

2 unpeeled kiwis, ends trimmed
2 green bell peppers, stemmed and seeded
3 (8-inch) celery stalks
1 (1-inch) knob of ginger, peeled
1 ounce fresh lemon juice
1 ounce fresh lime juice
1 ounce yellow Chartreuse
1 ounce gin

 In a blender, combine all the ingredients. Blend on high speed until smooth, about 30 seconds. Serve immediately in a tall glass, or chill in the refrigerator for 1 hour if you want a cold drink.

As Seen On . . .

TGIF
(Thank God It's Fizzy)

To me there was no hotter ticket than the Friday night programming block known as TGIF (Thank Goodness It's Funny, derived, obviously, from Thank God It's Friday) that aired on ABC straight through the '90s, from 1989 to 2000. Throughout its various iterations, the block contained hits like *Full House*, *Step by Step*, *Family Matters*, *Perfect Strangers*, and *Dinosaurs*. It eventually spawned (and is still spawning . . .) spinoffs, too.

Then or now, nothing quite matches the feeling of a Friday night sleepover with your BFFs as you settle in for two straight hours of sitcoms. If you ask me, root beer floats are the absolute pinnacle of sleepover decadence. This version is adulted-up with a maple-bourbon no-egg ice cream topped with bitters and chocolate sauce. As with all alcohol-spiked frozen treats, you need to keep the alcohol levels low in order to get a proper consistency.

2 scoops Maple-Bourbon Vanilla
   Ice Cream (recipe follows)
6 ounces root beer

1 ounce chocolate sauce
10 dashes Angostura bitters

Generously scoop the ice cream into a tall glass. Pour the root beer over the top. Just before serving, top with the chocolate sauce and bitters. Serve with a bubble tea straw and spoon.

Maple-Bourbon Vanilla Ice Cream
Makes about 2 cups

1 cup heavy cream
1 cup whole milk
1/4 cup dark maple syrup
1/2 vanilla bean, seeds scraped, or
   1/2 teaspoon pure vanilla extract
1/4 cup bourbon

In a medium airtight container, combine the cream, milk, and maple syrup. Whisk to combine completely. Add the vanilla seeds to the mixture,

cover, and chill in the refrigerator for at least 4 or up to 24 hours. Churn the mixture in an ice cream machine according to the manufacturer's instructions. When the mixture is nearly solid, slowly stir in the bourbon. Continue churning for 5 more minutes, then transfer to a clean container and freeze for at least 1 hour. Store the ice cream in an airtight container in the freezer for up to 2 weeks.

Saved by the Bellini

The influence that *Saved by the Bell* had on me cannot be overstated. I wanted Zack Morris's cool-guy personality, I wanted Kelly Kapowski's popularity, I wanted A. C. Slater's physique, I wanted Jessie Spano's GPA, and I wanted Lisa Turtle's credit card. The show is chock-full of out-of-control moments, like when Zack made a fake ID and managed to date a college-aged woman; Screech's sentient robot; Jessie's caffeine pills; and Lisa's broken leg dance. Remember when they tried to build an oil rig on school property, and somehow this gang of kids managed to stop it by using a duck?

Kind of like life at Bayside High, the Bellini can be sneakily tricky. Its construction is not particularly complicated, but it does rely on white peach purée, which isn't exactly widely available. You need to have it shipped frozen or live in a place with a fancy specialty shop. So, in the absence of Zack Morris's time-stopping superpowers (was he an alien?), I've devised a workaround that uses canned peaches, which are always in season everywhere. Prosecco is the classic choice for this drink, thanks to how its sharpness and acidity cut through the peaches' sweetness.

6 ounces Prosecco, chilled
1½ ounces Fake ID Peach Purée (recipe follows)
GARNISH: LIME WHEEL

 In a wine glass or large cocktail coupe, combine the drink ingredients. Stir gently to combine. Garnish with a lime wheel.

Fake ID Peach Purée
Makes about 2 cups

1 (15.25-ounce) can peaches with syrup
2 small ripe bananas
1 ounce fresh lime juice

In a blender, combine the peaches, bananas, and lime juice and blend on high speed until smooth, about 30 seconds. Strain into an airtight container through a wide-mesh strainer to separate out any large chunks and obtain a smoother texture. Store covered in the refrigerator for up to 2 weeks or in the freezer for up to 2 months.

As Seen On . . .

Honey Don't Play That

Watching *In Living Color* as a child meant that most of the humor went over my head. I'm not sure I realized it at the time, but a Black-led comedy show was revolutionary. It launched the careers of the Wayans family, along with David Alan Grier and Jim Carey. One of the most memorable sketches featured Homey D. Clown, an exasperated clown-for-hire played by Damon Wayans who, while dispensing questionable life lessons, spat out the catchphrase "Homey don't play that!" to register his disapproval. This was likely the show's most iconic catchphrase and character, appearing in nearly a dozen sketches throughout the show's three-season run.

As a show, *In Living Color* was an eclectic combination of comedy, hip-hop dance (shoutout to Fly Girls Rosie Perez and Jennifer Lopez), and social commentary. Along the same lines, this semi-tropical drink interestingly—and appealingly—mixes date-infused rum with fruit liqueurs, pineapple, chamomile, honey, and French grape brandy to make a frisky concoction. Honey is a great way to add a playful element to drinks as an alternative sweetener to boring simple syrup.

1 ounce Date-Infused Goslings Rum (page 67)
1 ounce pineapple juice, preferably fresh
¾ ounce fresh lime juice
½ ounce banana liqueur
½ ounce Cognac
½ ounce Turbo Honey Syrup (recipe opposite)
3 dashes Angostura bitters
GARNISH: PINEAPPLE LEAF

 In a shaker, combine the drink ingredients. Add ice and shake vigorously for 15 seconds. Strain into a tropical mug filled with ice. Garnish with the pineapple leaf and serve with a straw.

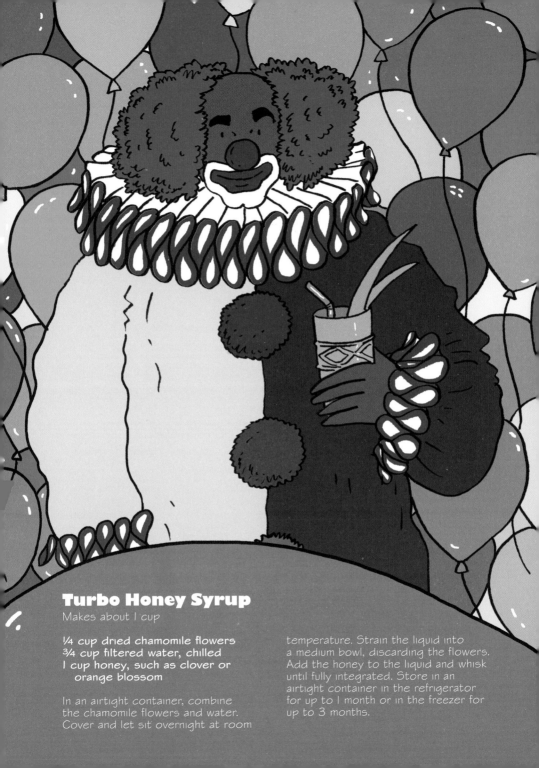

Turbo Honey Syrup

Makes about 1 cup

¼ cup dried chamomile flowers
¾ cup filtered water, chilled
1 cup honey, such as clover or
   orange blossom

In an airtight container, combine
the chamomile flowers and water.
Cover and let sit overnight at room
temperature. Strain the liquid into
a medium bowl, discarding the flowers.
Add the honey to the liquid and whisk
until fully integrated. Store in an
airtight container in the refrigerator
for up to 1 month or in the freezer for
up to 3 months.

The Ritual

1999. It was a wild year at the movies. The *Star Wars* prequel trilogy began, *The Matrix* was released, as well as *Election, Boys Don't Cry, Eyes Wide Shut, Office Space* . . . But the one that changed the way we think about cinema, and even our relationship to media, is *The Blair Witch Project*. Made on a tiny budget with no-name actors and barely a script at all, the film's marketing gimmick was positioning it as found footage from a doomed documentary effort rather than as a work of make-believe. The cast encountered talismans and eventually met an unspecified—but decidedly not appealing—fate in the basement of an abandoned house where the Blair Witch allegedly resided.

Much like the instantly iconic spooky figurines strewn about the forest by the film's producers, these flaming, cinnamon-impaled oranges will scare you. Use cider made in America or France that contains alcohol but is still sweet and fruity, as opposed to a funky, dry Spanish style. Or you can lower the overall proof with a nonalcoholic sparkling cider.

ORANGE GARNISH
3 medium navel oranges, washed
3 cinnamon sticks
30 dried cloves
1 cup overproof rum

PUNCH
1 (750mL) bottle sparkling cider
4 cups apple cider
10 ounces blended Scotch whisky
5 ounces Bénédictine
5 ounces allspice liqueur

Preheat the oven to 350°F. Line a baking sheet with foil.

Make the orange garnish. Impale each orange with 1 cinnamon stick, threading it through, and stud each with 8 to 10 cloves. Arrange the adorned oranges on the prepared baking sheet and roast until oozing, 15 to 20 minutes. Transfer the oranges to a wire rack to cool for about 10 minutes, then place in a large, shallow bowl. Pour the rum over the oranges and let soak for at least 15 minutes and up to 45 minutes.

Meanwhile, make the punch. In a large bowl, combine the drink ingredients with 4 to 5 cups of ice. Stir to combine.

When ready to serve, ignite the rum-soaked oranges and, using heat-proof tongs, place them in the bowl. Ladle the punch into glasses to serve.

D&D

Melrose Place holds a special spot in my heart because it's one of the first TV shows I can remember portraying a gay person. Thankfully, that's been normalized on primetime networks in the last few decades, but it was a radical act at the time. The Aaron Spelling–produced show, hugely popular and running for seven seasons, was radical in other ways, too. For two seasons, conceptual artist Mel Chin collaborated with set designer Deborah Seigel to subtly incorporate his collective's art into set elements and props. They snuck in details like sheets with unrolled condoms printed on them, pool table sets commenting on racism, and custom liquor bottles depicting the history of alcohol. In 1997, the works appeared in a real show at LA's Museum of Contemporary Art (MOCA), which *Melrose Place*'s characters attended as part of filming. Heather Locklear's fictional ad agency, D&D, takes on MOCA as a client—yes, a fake agency took on a real museum giving real publicity to a real show. You still with me? Ultimately Locklear's character takes over the agency, renaming it Amanda Woodward Advertising—big M&A energy.

In this instance, D&D is very real—it stands for Dark & Datey, and it's a riff on the classic Dark 'n' Stormy. In a similarly self-referential act as what's described here, this variation incorporates dried dates to give a spicy-yet-refreshing drink an extra balmy feel.

2 ounces Date-Infused Goslings Rum (recipe opposite)
¾ ounce fresh lime juice
¾ ounce Ginger Syrup (page 54)
3 ounces sparkling water
GARNISHES: RUM-SOAKED DATE (SEE OPPOSITE), LIME WHEEL, GINGER CANDY

 In a shaker, combine the rum, lime juice, and ginger syrup. Shake quickly to combine. Pour into a hurricane glass filled with ice and top with the sparkling water. Garnish with the rum-soaked date, lime wheel, and ginger candy on a pick.

Date-Infused Goslings Rum

Makes about 10 ounces rum, plus 8 rum-soaked dates

8 dried, pitted dates
12 ounces Goslings rum

In an airtight container, combine the dates and rum. Cover and let soak at room temperature overnight. Strain the liquid through a fine-mesh strainer into a clean container. Lay out the soaked dates on a paper towel to dry for at least 4 hours, then transfer them to a separate airtight container. Store the infused rum in a cool, dark place for up to 1 month; store the dates in a cool, dark place for up to 1 week.

Blood and Sand and Goosebumps

R. L. Stine's infamous Goosebumps series, first launched in 1992, tells serialized stories of kids shocked and awed into scary, unexpected situations. The shiny, textured, dripping text on the book covers was instantly recognizable, and with more than sixty books all-in, they were highly collectible. Surreal (and sometimes supernatural) horror for kids—it makes perfect sense. The series went on to yield TV shows, movies, comic books, and so much more media.

The classic Blood and Sand cocktail is as terrifying as those Goosebumps books are to preteens. When I was behind the bar, I always lived in terror of someone ordering one. On paper, it looks delicious, but they always come out limp and underwhelming because orange juice lacks the concentrated acidity of other citruses like lemon and lime. Over the years, I've made attempts to perfect it, but it's always ended in tears. Ultimately, to me, the Goosebumps books are about facing your fears and learning bravery. This recipe is my final, valorous attempt to fix this drink, once and for all.

2 ounces blended Scotch whisky
¾ ounce Cherry Heering
1 ounce Ultragrenadine (page 71)
½ ounce fresh orange juice
¼ ounce fresh lemon juice
GARNISH: LUXARDO CHERRIES

 In a shaker, combine all the drink ingredients. Add ice and shake vigorously for 15 seconds. Strain into a cocktail coupe. Garnish with Luxardo cherries on a pick.

As Seen On . . .

Dark Phoenix

The opening riff of the *X-Men* animated series theme song is seared into my mind. This show, which first aired in 1992 and ran for five seasons, resonated with me personally because I had (have) a penchant for futuristic shows with superpowered beings. But it also resonated with me as an allegory for the queer experience: the mutants of *X-Men* were at once revered and reviled for their fabulous superhuman abilities, much like how, in the real world, queer people are celebrated as iconoclastic cultural vanguards by some and seen as deviant threats by others.

Season three's arc saw the psychic mutant Jean Grey transforming into the Dark Phoenix when she merges with an alien being and becomes out-of-control powerful. Instead of spoiling the ending, I'll offer you a drink that relies on layering heavier and more dense liquids beneath lighter ones to create a gradient effect just like Dark Phoenix's iconic fiery aura.

2 ounces Ultragrenadine (recipe opposite)
1 ounce fresh orange juice
1 ounce vodka
3 ounces sparkling water
GARNISH: ORANGE WHEEL

Fill a tall glass with ice. First layer in the Ultragrenadine, then the orange juice, followed by the vodka. Top the drink with the sparkling water—do not stir. Garnish with the orange wheel.

Notes:

- You can skip the saffron infusion in the Ultragrenadine recipe, and just use the filtered water instead.
- If you must, you can use regular grenadine anywhere this recipe is called for; your drink will be fine, but I cannot promise it will be ultradelicious.

Ultragrenadine

Makes about 5 cups

¼ teaspoon saffron threads
   (optional; see Notes)
2 cups filtered water
2 black tea bags
2 cups granulated sugar
1 cup 100% pomegranate juice, such
   as POM
1 cup 100% cranberry juice, such as
   RW Knudsen

In a small airtight container, combine the saffron with 1 cup of the filtered water. Cover and let sit at room temperature overnight. Meanwhile, in a separate small airtight container, pour the remaining 1 cup filtered water over the tea bags. Let sit, covered, overnight as well.

Strain the liquid from both infusions into a medium saucepan, discarding the saffron threads and tea bags. Add the sugar and both juices. Place the pan over medium-low heat and cook, stirring constantly, until the sugar is dissolved, about 5 minutes. Store in an airtight container in the refrigerator for up to 1 month or in the freezer for up to 3 months.

toys,
technology
&
games

DISCOVERY ZONE

The Away Message

I was fortunate enough to grow up with a dad who was as big of a computer nerd as I am. As a result, I had access to the information superhighway pretty early on in its rollout. My family signed on to America Online in 1997, thus gaining access to one of the earliest wonders of the World Wide Web: instant messaging. While one of the best parts of the '90s was that you could be completely unreachable for hours or even days and everyone was okay with it, you could, alternatively, put up an away message to tell other users what you were doing away from your parents' Macintosh Quadra. Some messages were straightforward ("Rollerblading with Zuki!"), but hidden meanings, ~~*SoNg LyRiCs*~~, and inside jokes were aplenty. My favorites were those that referenced being at a party I wasn't invited to.

Quite simply, this drink is based on the AIM acronym—a great if slightly weird internet program that translates into a great if slightly weird drink. It will definitely hit the spot if you're settling in for a long night of chatting.

1 ounce aquavit
1 ounce Irish whiskey
1 ounce Midori

 In a mixing glass or shaking tin, combine all the ingredients. Add ice and stir gently for 20 seconds. Strain into an old fashioned glass filled with ice.

The Apple Mac-Tini

The '90s were a transformative decade for consumer electronics. Computers went from being bulky, decidedly unsexy boxes, usually kept out of sight behind cabinets or in dedicated "computer rooms," to genuinely beautiful pieces of industrial design. Like many transformations, this one was in large part thanks to Apple. At the beginning of the decade, the company floundered, pumping out bland, dull boxes. But then Steve Jobs tasked designer Jonathan Ive with beautifying the all-in-one iMac computer. Released in 1998, it completely and forever changed how people believed computers should look. This piece of machinery, available in six vibrantly translucent colors—including a striking lime green—was something you wanted to show off.

Batched cocktails like this one represent a similar win for efficiency and good looks. You can prep this riff on the Appletini (a '90s icon in its own right) ahead of time, and thanks to the lime juice, the drink will keep its vibrant green hue long after your old computer dies from playing too many rounds of Prince of Persia.

10 ounces gin or vodka

6 ounces dry vermouth

1 ounce fresh lime juice

1 tablespoon granulated sugar

1 large unpeeled green apple, cored and roughly chopped

5 ounces filtered water, chilled

In a blender, combine the gin, vermouth, lime juice, sugar, and apple. Blend on high until the apple is liquefied, about 30 seconds. Strain the mixture through a fine-mesh strainer into a large bowl. In an airtight container, combine the strained apple mixture and filtered water. Chill in the refrigerator for at least 2 hours.

When ready to serve, pour into cocktail coupes. Store any extra mixture in the refrigerator for up to 2 weeks or in the freezer (see Note) for up to 2 months.

Note: When serving from the freezer, allow the drink to sit at room temperature for 10 minutes before pouring.

Egg Watch

If I spent half as much time on my homework as I did seeking out—and then playing with—a Tamagotchi, I would have probably been the valedictorian of my middle school. The Tamagotchi was cool as hell, so I regret nothing. This toy, released in 1997, was a cutesy keychain that contained a tiny computer whose sole purpose was to display an interactive "pet." You were supposed to feed, play with, and clean up after the little creature until it died of natural causes and went to digital heaven. The Tamagotchi was one of the first digital toys to offer play experiences that could re-create life in some limited way.

The word *tamagotchi* is a Japanese portmanteau of the words for *egg* and *watch*, so, obviously, it deserves an egg-based cocktail in its name. Think of this drink as a quick, somewhat fruity eggnog, perfect for a cool evening indoors cleaning up digital dookie from your pixelated pet.

2 ounces tawny port
1 ounce Chambord
1 large egg
GARNISH: FRESH NUTMEG

 In a shaker, combine the drink ingredients and shake for 5 seconds to integrate the egg. Add ice and shake vigorously for 15 seconds. Strain the drink into a large cocktail coupe. Grate the nutmeg over the top to finish.

Tae Blue

The way Tae Bo and its creator, Billy Blanks, swept the nation in the '90s was remarkable. Tae Bo was Blanks's fusion of Korean kickboxing (tae kwon do) and American boxing. He actually developed it in the '80s, but the fitness trend did not take off with certainty until the late '90s when commercials for at-home VHS workout tapes saturated the airwaves. Blanks became a bona fide celebrity, showing up on Oprah's talk show and in countless magazine and newspaper profiles.

In addition to its martial arts, Korea has many amazing exports, one of them being drinkable, sweetened yogurt, and another being soju, an inexpensive low-ABV spirit that resembles a slightly more flavorful vodka. This DIY drinkable yogurt (Yoplait's Go-Gurt also debuted in 1997, by the way) is low enough in alcohol not to be a terrible post-workout beverage, but I might save it for dessert.

¼ cup plain nonfat yogurt
3 ounces soju
¾ ounce Chambord

 In a shaker, combine all the ingredients. Add ice and shake vigorously for 15 seconds. Strain into a cocktail coupe.

SCORE 20
TIME 0:40
RINGS 16

Casino Night Daisy

In 1989, my older brother got the Nintendo Entertainment System, and Mario and his friends practically became members of our family. But as the '90s boomed and the console wars heated up, Sega Genesis began to reign supreme. I had to have it—and I was lucky enough to get it. My first game? *Sonic: The Hedgehog,* obviously. The primary difference between Mario and Sonic was in the design: Mario navigated linear mazes that required precise jumping, while Sonic required speed and vertical motion. Sonic's levels could be accomplished on lower tracks that were a bit easier to reach, or upper tracks that were riskier but more rewarding. The Casino Night Zone from *Sonic 2* felt as tall as it was long, and it portrayed a glittering world of excess.

The Sonic franchise was all about fun, speed, and vibrant color palates, and Sonic's cobalt fur lends itself perfectly to this blue-hued, berry-inflected margarita riff. Had I been of drinking age in the early '90s, I might have knocked back a couple of these as I made my way toward Dr. Robotnik's lair.

1½ ounces blanco tequila
¾ ounce fresh lemon juice
¾ ounce blue curaçao
½ ounce Chambord
GARNISH: LEMON WHEEL

In a shaker, combine the drink ingredients. Add ice and shake vigorously for 15 seconds. Strain into a cocktail coupe. Garnish with the lemon wheel—bonus point if it's mangled and spiky and kind of looks like Super Sonic.

The Dream Phone

Who who who's got a crush on you? As a young gay kid in the '90s, I would have relished the opportunity to have openly discussed my budding romantic desires with friends over a game of Electronic Dream Phone, but alas. This now-defunct board game was somewhat similar to the more enduring Guess Who in that you used clues to guess someone's identity; in the instance of the former, however, these clues were of course delivered to you on a hot pink phone, and you were guessing which guy in school had a crush on you. It was a girly girl fantasy through-and-through.

Such a game, of course, requires a pink and girly drink to go along with it. This one features a strawberry-kiwi blend (one of the most '90s combos ever—just recall your Lip Smackers collection or Snapple's offerings) along with rose liqueur, vodka, and sparkling rosé. G2G, 1992 is calling . . . on my dream phone.

1 ounce Cowabunga Sauce (recipe
   follows)
1 ounce vodka
½ ounce rose liqueur
¾ ounce fresh lemon juice

¼ ounce Heart in a Blender Simple
   Syrup (page 141)
3 ounces sparkling rosé, chilled
GARNISH: DRIED ROSE PETALS

In a shaker, combine the Cowabunga Sauce, vodka, rose liqueur, lemon juice, and simple syrup. Add ice and shake vigorously for 15 seconds. Strain into a cocktail coupe and top with the sparkling wine. Garnish with the dried rose petals.

Cowabunga Sauce
Makes about 12 ounces

2 unpeeled ripe kiwis, ends trimmed
1 (12 ounce) bottle strawberry
   liqueur

In a blender, combine the kiwis and strawberry liqueur. Blend on high for 1 minute, until completely liquefied. Strain the mixture through a fine-mesh strainer into an airtight container. Store the infused liqueur in the refrigerator for up to 2 months.

The Slammer

Milk Caps is a game that was being played on every single playground in the '90s—you might have known it as Pogs. Players stack cardboard bottle caps and, using a plastic or rubber implement known as a "slammer," try to flip over and collect as many caps as possible in order to win. Pogs is a reference to the Hawaiian drink made from passionfruit, orange, and guava with a cap that was widely used to play. The game can be traced back centuries to countries in Asia like Japan and the Philippines.

The original Pog juice can be tough to find everywhere, but we can re-create its flavor trifecta with off-the-shelf guava and passionfruit nectar, while juicing readily available oranges to give that bit of freshness. (If you're able to use fresh guava and/or passionfruit juice, be my guest.) This drink works perfectly fine without the spirits, but the unlikely pairing of citrus vodka, rum, and tequila gives this drink a subtle yet intriguing complexity.

3 cups ice
1 cup passionfruit nectar
1 cup guava nectar
1 cup fresh orange juice
1 ounce citron vodka
1 ounce blanco tequila
1 ounce dark rum
GARNISH: ORANGE WHEELS

In a blender, combine the drink ingredients. Blend on medium until smooth, about 10 seconds. Pour into tall glasses. Garnish each with an orange wheel and serve with bubble tea straws.

The Ballzooka

I am a committed pacifist (I've never even been in a fist fight!), but that didn't stop me from going all in for Nerf guns when I was eleven years old. It was fashionable among my group of friends to host "Nerf War" sleepover parties for our birthdays. My favorite weapon was the Ballzooka—I literally slept with it. It was a massive cannon that could launch fifteen yellow Nerf balls in quick succession.

While I'd love to soak a Nerf ball in rum and call it a day, actually edible tapioca pearls—known throughout Asia as boba—make a much better choice. You'll commonly find them in dark colors, but you can buy green tea–flavored pearls and soak them in Midori so that they take on that perfect, famous green-yellow hue. Combine that with Mountain Dew, high-proof rum, and blue curaçao, and you've got a tween's idea of a cool cocktail. No shame.

⅓ cup green tea tapioca pearls
½ cup Midori
1½ ounces overproof Jamaican rum
¾ ounce blue curaçao
½ ounce fresh lime juice
2 ounces Mountain Dew

 Prepare the tapioca pearls according to the package directions, but instead of cooling them in water, use the Midori. Let the pearls absorb the liqueur for 15 to 20 minutes until green-yellow in color.

Place the soaked tapioca pearls in the bottom of an old fashioned glass, then fill with ice.

In a shaker, combine the rum, blue curaçao, and lime juice. Add ice and shake vigorously for 15 seconds. Strain into the prepared glass and then top with the Mountain Dew. Serve with a bubble tea straw.

Serra Angel

Summon Angel

Flying
Does not tap when attacking.

Born with wings of light and a sword of faith, this heavenly incarnation embodies both fury and purity.

4/4

Serra Angel

Magic: The Gathering hit me and my friends hard. We already had a predisposition to collectible cardboard through our love of Marvel cards, so when this fantasy combat game hit shelves in 1993, we just about lost it. The game featured five genres of magic, each aligned with a particular color. Red was fire and destruction; green was growth and power; black meant death and pain; blue was the realm of illusion and trickery; and white was peace and holy might. The Serra Angel, a white creature card, had special abilities like flying—and though it was not extremely rare, it was sought after nonetheless.

The rules of Magic are too complicated for me to consider drinking a cocktail while playing, but those with more cognitive fortitude might want to stir this one up for their next match. This drink bears a slight resemblance to a Vesper, with the sherry standing in for vermouth, and Bénédictine liqueur offering a frisson of monastic, herbal energy.

1 ounce gin
1½ ounces Fino sherry
¼ ounce Bénédictine
2 dashes orange bitters

 In a mixing glass or shaking tin, combine all the ingredients. Add ice and stir gently for 20 seconds. Strain into a cocktail coupe.

Home Keys

makes
1 drink

I still have stress dreams about the computer game *Mavis Beacon Teaches Typing*. Despite allegedly being a writer, my typing skills are abysmal and probably only in the mid double digits in terms of words per minute. Nevertheless, I have a deep fondness for the reigning queen of the home keys on the QWERTY keyboard . . . a fondness that shattered only a little bit after learning that Mavis Beacon is not even a real person.

The learning tool (disguised as a game) was all about peak performance and precise focus in order to increase your words per minute and keep typos low, which is why I would never recommend drinking alcohol while learning how to type. But this oddly fruity coffee drink has just the right amount of caffeine and complexity to sustain even the most strident typing session.

1½ ounces filtered water, chilled
1½ ounces cold brew coffee concentrate
¾ ounce Ultragrenadine (page 71)

In a mixing glass or shaking tin, combine all the ingredients. Add ice and stir gently for 20 seconds. Strain into a cocktail coupe.

Hyrule Highball

The first *Legend of Zelda* video game came out at the tail end of the 1980s, but the franchise really took off when the sequel, *The Legend of Zelda: A Link to the Past*, was released in 1992. This game blew everyone's minds with its stellar graphics and innovative open-world game design. Hyrule is the name of the land in which most Zelda games are set. It is a place filled with lush greenery, treacherous mountains, perilous deserts, and idyllic beaches. The dramatic intro sequence where Link, the game's hero, is awoken in the rain and called upon to rescue a princess trapped in Hyrule Castle is still one of my true "happy places" that I envision during, say, a particularly excruciating dentist visit.

If Link and I were to share a drink in this digital wonderland, it would be this riff on a highball that represents the diversity (and dangers) of the land of Hyrule. Yes, the combination of spirits is daunting, but this verdant cocktail gives rise to an emergent, refreshing landscape that you'll want to get lost in.

2 ounces Mountain Dew
¾ ounce fresh lime juice
½ ounce vodka
½ ounce gin
½ ounce white rum
½ ounce blanco tequila

½ ounce Midori
½ ounce Cointreau
¼ ounce Heart in a Blender Simple
  Syrup (page 141)

GARNISHES: LIME WHEEL, HONEYDEW BALL, LUXARDO CHERRY

Fill a tall glass with ice and add 1 ounce of the Mountain Dew.

In a shaker, combine the lime juice, vodka, gin, rum, tequila, Midori, Cointreau, and simple syrup. Fill the shaker with ice and shake vigorously for 15 seconds. Strain into the prepared glass, then layer the remaining 1 ounce Mountain Dew over the top.

Garnish with the lime wheel, melon ball, and Luxardo cherry on a pick. Serve with a straw.

Furby-dden Fruit

Consumer marketing in the '90s was a landscape of promises that never panned out. The Future felt like it was right around the corner, and the Furby—a "sentient" toy—was one of those things that promised to be more than it actually was. The toy was supposed to start off speaking a nonsense language—Furbish—before "picking up" human phrases. This change didn't occur via a complex language processing technology; rather, the toy just started speaking English on a timer. But the marketing was so convincing that the NSA banned them on their property for fear they were covert listening devices.

While we don't have bartending robots just yet, we can mix up a cocktail ourselves that's a fitting tribute to the Furby's mythical intelligence. This semi-slushie drink is based on a forbidden fruit syrup appearing in late-twentieth-century bar books that's mostly grapefruit. Combined with fresh basil and St-Germain, you get a refreshing and complex treat that lives up to the hype. Best of all, you can store the mixture in the freezer for up to two weeks.

1½ cups filtered water
1½ cups granulated sugar
Zest of two grapefruits
1 cup fresh grapefruit juice
½ ounce fresh lemon juice

½ ounce fresh lime juice
1 cup loosely packed whole basil
   leaves, plus more for garnish
4 ounces pisco
4 ounces St-Germain

In a food processor or blender, combine the water, sugar, grapefruit zest, grapefruit juice, lemon juice, and lime juice. Blend on high until the sugar is completely dissolved, about 45 seconds. Stir in the basil leaves. Transfer to an airtight container and chill in the refrigerator for at least 3 hours or up to 12 hours.

Strain the liquid through a fine-mesh strainer, discarding the solids, then churn in an ice cream machine according to the manufacturer's directions. Once nearly solid, pour in the pisco and St-Germain and churn again for at least 5 more minutes. Serve immediately or transfer to the freezer to harden for at least 3 hours or up to 12 hours.

Pour into tall glasses and garnish with more basil leaves. Serve with bubble tea straws and spoons.

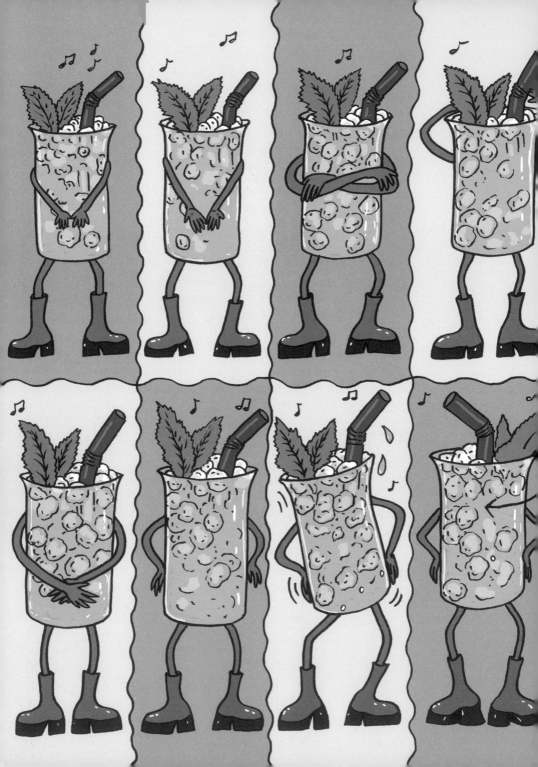

Ay Mockarena

Before we had TikTok dance challenges, we had the Macarena. It was a four-step dance routine that required little to no effort and could be performed by just about anyone (including a bunch of overly exuberant Democratic leaders at the 1996 Democratic National Convention—look it up, it's wild). The song we all know, love, and now have stuck in our heads at its mere mention is a remix of a Spanish duo Los Del Río song by a group known as the Bayside Boys. In addition to incorporating a sample of the iconic laugh from synth pop band Yaz's "Situation," they also added an English vocal track that's pretty dirty if you stop dancing for a sec to listen to the words. It tells the story of a woman who, bored of her current boyfriend, fools around with his two friends.

Like music, some of the best cocktails are the ones that are secretly dirty. The hit of savory from olive brine—usually reserved for dirty martinis— takes this mocktail from fruity and sweet to perfectly balanced. The added science-nerd bonus is that the salt from the brine lowers the freezing point of the juices and makes the drink super, stingingly cold. It's perfect for cooling off after that dance in your middle school cafeteria.

4 ounces mango nectar, such as Rica or Ceres
3 ounces fresh orange juice
¾ ounce fresh lime juice
½ ounce olive brine
GARNISH: MINT SPRIGS

In a shaker, combine the drink ingredients. Add ice and shake vigorously for 15 seconds. Strain into a tall glass filled with ice. Garnish with the mint sprigs and serve with a straw.

style
&
fashion

MALL MADNESS

Smells Like Teen Spirit

I have purchased two bottles of cologne in my entire life; Acqua di Gio was one of them in 1997. For fifteen-year-old me, cologne was part of a package of items like skater clothes and hacky sacks that helped me sell the lie that I was not flamingly gay. Buying the blatantly homoerotic, muscle-bound, torso-shaped Jean Paul Gaultier cologne put me at risk of outing myself, so I resigned myself to the Armani fragrance instead.

I think we can all agree that Acqua di Gio is simply how the '90s smelled. The cologne has predominant notes of citrus, so this Italian-ish margarita feels appropriate. Amaretto is an almond liqueur that gets a bad rap these days, but when used appropriately and judiciously, it can add an unexpected richness and depth . . . just like Acqua di Gio.

1¾ ounces reposado tequila
¾ ounce amaretto
¾ ounce fresh lime juice
½ ounce fresh orange juice
¼ ounce Heart in a Blender Simple Syrup (page 141)
GARNISH: LIME WEDGE

In a shaker, combine the drink ingredients. Add ice and shake vigorously for 15 seconds. Strain into an old fashioned glass with one large ice cube or a cocktail coupe. Garnish with the lime wedge.

Side-Snap Thirst Quencher

Before we had athleisure as we know it today, we had the sporty aesthetic of the '90s. Sports weren't just something you did; they were a lifestyle you embodied, whether or not you were actually playing any. Umbro shorts, sports bras in public (thank you, Brandi Chastain) . . . these were items you could just wear without needing to justify that you were on your way to practice. If you didn't have a pair of Adidas tearaway track pants with snaps all the way down the leg that you could rip off in five seconds flat, I hope, for your sake, that you just stayed home.

The sporty aesthetic also seeped its way into our drinking habits. Obviously, you needed some Gatorade to go along with your outfit. The "sports drink" was billed as a magical rehydrator after a draining workout, even though it's just sorta-salty sugar water with food coloring. This drink pairs blue Gatorade (my favorite flavor, personally) with herbal yellow Chartreuse to give a simple, athletic-adjacent cocktail that's perfect for when you're in the stands watching someone else kick around a ball.

4½ ounces blue Gatorade
1½ ounces yellow Chartreuse
GARNISH: ORANGE WEDGE

In a shaker, combine the drink ingredients. Add ice and shake vigorously for 15 seconds. Pour the entire contents of the shaker, including the ice, into a plastic cup. Garnish with the orange wedge, preferably warm and out of a plastic bag.

Slap Wrap

The slap bracelet is the first fashion fad I remember. When I was in second grade, everyone had them. For me, a budding gay, a brightly colored, shape-shifting accessory was irresistible. (Fun fact: the actual brand name is Slap Wrap, which sounds like a made-up sex move you'd find in *Cosmopolitan*.) Unfortunately, like all the very best things in this life, slap bracelets were banned pretty quickly. Turns out that when the fabric sheath fell off the metal, people started cutting themselves. My eight-year-old aesthetic never really recovered.

Fortunately, there's a drink for that. This low-proof vermouth-based cocktail is made with lemon and tangerine juice (or orange in a pinch) to give it a "slap" of acidity. Plus, you can trim your tangerine peel into the shape of a bracelet and run no risk of injury.

2 ounces dry vermouth
1 ounce fresh tangerine juice
½ ounce fresh lemon juice
¼ ounce crème de cacao
GARNISH: EXTRA-LONG TANGERINE PEEL

 In a shaker, combine the drink ingredients. Add ice and shake vigorously for 15 seconds. Strain into a cocktail coupe. Garnish with the tangerine peel, cut into the shape of a slap bracelet.

The Pumps

The real-world consolation prize for not having Marty McFly's awesome sneakers from *Back to the Future 2* were Reebok's Pumps. Apparently, the built-in air pumps, shaped and designed like basketballs, would force air into the shoes to make them fit more snugly. But the sneakers also had laces, which is confusing. These shoes were pure '90s over-the-top absurd materialism masquerading as functionality. I loved them and had *at least* one pair.

What better way to celebrate this quintessential un-useless shoe than with an equally absurd drink? But don't be intimidated by the tapioca pearls—they're easy to find and a cinch to prepare. And just like inflatable shoes, they are completely unnecessary but so much fun.

½ cup tapioca pearls
3 ounces fresh watermelon juice
1 ounce blanco tequila
1 ounce raspberry liqueur
1 ounce banana liqueur
¾ ounce fresh lime juice
¼ ounce absinthe
2 ounces sparkling water

In a tall glass, rehydrate the tapioca pearls according to the package directions.

Meanwhile, in a shaker, combine the watermelon juice, tequila, raspberry and banana liqueurs, lime juice, and absinthe. Add ice and shake vigorously for 15 seconds. Strain into the prepared glass over the rehydrated tapioca pearls. Fill the glass with ice and top with the sparkling water. Serve with a bubble tea straw.

Flannel Factor

We can't talk about fashion in the '90s without talking about grunge, and we can't talk about grunge without talking about flannel. The fabric was everywhere: movies, bed sheets, pajama pants given out at bar/ bat mitzvahs . . . but no form of flannel was more popular than that of the flannel shirt. If you threw one on—maybe unbuttoned with a T-shirt underneath or maybe tied around your waist—and put your feet in a pair of Dr. Martens, you'd give off an air of ambivalence and effortlessness that pervaded the zeitgeist. You didn't want to look like you tried too hard, but people still wanted to look put together. You wanted to look like Jared Leto in *My So-Called Life*. The flannel shirt gave—hell, still gives—a perfect blend of comfort and ruggedness, and just enough formality to look good while still acting "whatever."

The most indelible expression of '90s flannel—to me at least—is the classic red-and-black Buffalo Plaid flannel shirt. It had the right balance of moody and vibrant, not unlike this drink. The barrel-aged spirits offer a brooding depth, balanced by the acidity (and caffeine) from the cold brew concentrate, rounded out by some confectionary notes from the amaretto. Topped with decadent Luxardo cherries, this cocktail shows up to the party on time but never looks like it's trying too hard.

1 ounce dark rum
1 ounce rye
1 ounce cold brew coffee concentrate
1 ounce amaretto
GARNISH: 3 LUXARDO CHERRIES

 In a mixing glass or shaking tin, combine the drink ingredients. Add ice and stir gently for 20 seconds. Pour into an old fashioned glass filled with ice and garnish with the Luxardo cherries on a pick.

STRUCTURE

When I started buying my own clothes, I spent a lot of time at the mall strolling past the windows of such bulwarks of '90s fashion as Hollister, Abercrombie & Fitch, Aeropostale, and PacSun; my personal North Star was STRUCTURE. I preferred the brand's more streamlined, semi-futuristic offerings to the preppy, surfer, or vaguely European (or all of the above) vibes those others seemed to lean all the way into. Ultimately the brand was bought by Sears, and now it offers a sad selection of nondescript button-down shirts—online only. It was good while it lasted.

Like clothes, cocktails are also all about STRUCTURE. When you're mixing a drink, you want to create something that's built to be balanced. This hybrid of a Cape Codder and Salty Dog (two very preppy cocktails that definitely love their time by the beach) showcases this principle brilliantly. The salted rim counteracts the bitterness from the grapefruit juice, while the Ultragrenadine softens the juice's acidity. Aromatically, the layered complexity of the Ultragrenadine expands into the neutral vodka. Overthinking drinks *and* fashion . . . who, me?

Lime wedges
Kosher salt
2 ounces vodka
1 ounce fresh grapefruit juice
½ ounce Ultragrenadine (page 71)

Use a lime wedge to moisten the rim of an old fashioned glass. Dip the glass in the kosher salt to apply a thin layer of salt, shaking off any excess. Then fill the glass with ice. Add the vodka, grapefruit juice, and Ultragrenadine. Stir quickly just to combine. Garnish with another lime wedge.

Kitty Highball

I was well into my thirties when I first set foot in a Claire's boutique—and thank goodness these stores outlasted the '90s, because they are Valhalla for those who love hot pink and feathers. For the uninitiated, Claire's is a hyper-feminine wonderland of hair ties, jewelry, nail polish, and a lot more. If you didn't get your ears pierced at Claire's, did it even really happen?

To properly imbue your spirit with that of this sensational store, you'll want a playful, simple, and, yes, girly tall drink—and this one has just enough of a weird, gothy edge to keep you coming back for more (and to remind you that Hot Topic is probably the next store over). The Kitty Highball is an under-the-radar staple dating back to at least the '70s. More modern renditions have made the drink from ginger syrup and soda rather than off-the-shelf ginger ale, but, like all young tweens who secretly got up to no good at the mall, this drink rebels against type with the inclusion of a curiously earthy sesame syrup.

4 to 5 ounces ginger ale

3 ounces light red wine, such as pinot noir

½ ounce Kitty Syrup (recipe follows)

GARNISHES: GINGER CANDY AND A LUXARDO CHERRY

 In a tall glass filled with ice, combine the drink ingredients. Stir quickly to combine. Garnish with the ginger candy and Luxardo cherry on a pick. Serve with a straw.

Kitty Syrup

Makes about 1 cup

1 cup white sesame seeds
1 cup filtered water
½ cup granulated sugar

Preheat the oven to 350°F. On a baking sheet, spread out the sesame seeds. Toast until lightly golden and fragrant, 8 to 10 minutes. Transfer the toasted seeds to a medium saucepan. Add the water and stir to combine. Bring to a boil over medium heat, then reduce the heat to low and simmer until the liquid reduces by half, about 15 minutes; the seeds will be very soft, almost like oatmeal. With a fine-mesh strainer, strain the liquid from the seeds, discarding the seeds, and return the steeped liquid to the pan. Add the sugar to the warm liquid and stir to dissolve. Transfer to an airtight container and store in the refrigerator for up to 3 weeks or in the freezer for up to 3 months.

Wide Wide Wale

Yeah, I wore JNCO jeans. I'm not ashamed to admit it. Even though I never set foot on a skateboard (and I know my purple Rollerblades did not count), I gleefully appropriated skater fashion. I thought it was cool—and I bet you did too! I loved wide-leg jeans; they were comfortable and the walls of fabric that shrouded my skinny teenage legs added the perfect touch of drama to any outfit. Speaking of wide, wide-wale corduroy was another irresistible element of this particular brand of fashion. I had a pair of tan wide-leg, wide-wale JNCOs that I cherished—and frankly, wish I still owned.

This drink, wide in its depth, takes the classic Boulevardier recipe and adds mellow sesame syrup for a chill, down-to-earth vibe. I like to sip on one while I scour the country looking for any remaining GadZOOKS locations.

1½ ounces bourbon
½ ounce Campari
¾ ounce sweet vermouth
½ ounce Kitty Syrup (page 115)
GARNISH: ORANGE PEEL

In a mixing glass or shaking tin, combine the drink ingredients. Add ice and stir gently for 20 seconds. Strain into a cocktail coupe. Garnish with the orange peel, expressed and then perched on the rim.

Slinky Sipper

Few things scream *'90s!* more loudly than Steve Madden's chunky platform shoes. The white sneakers were really something (did you have the single- or double-decker?), but the stretch black sandals . . . well, they were everywhere from middle school hallways to Hollywood red carpets. And for good reason: they were extraordinarily versatile and easy to throw on, offering a semi-formal footwear option and embodying a desired rugged, practical femininity. These shoes managed to be girly without going over the top on a stereotyped gender role. Too bad I was not cool enough back in the '90s to rock a pair of these because I would have slayed.

With drinks, people also have a tendency to assign gender. But like the slinky sandal, this Scotch- and Cognac-based drink has some frissons of femininity while also spanning the spectrum. Herbal Bénédictine liqueur provides some pious complexity. The rose petals over the top are entirely optional, but I never pass up an opportunity to get dolled up.

¾ ounce Scotch whisky
¾ ounce Cognac
¾ ounce fresh lime juice
½ ounce Bénédictine
½ ounce rose liqueur
¼ ounce Heart in a Blender Simple Syrup (page 141)
1 egg white
OPTIONAL GARNISH: DRIED ROSE PETALS

 In a shaker, combine the drink ingredients. Shake briefly to integrate the egg white, then add ice and shake vigorously for 15 seconds. Strain into a large cocktail coupe. Garnish with the rose petals, if desired.

Frosted Tips

As someone with a deep commitment to dyeing his hair (but without a commitment to any particular color), I have a strong affection for the often-maligned '90s hair trend known as frosted tips. A high percentage of high-profile heartthrobs plastering bedroom walls featured them: at least one singer from every boy band, JTT, Joshua Jackson, Val Kilmer, Freddie Prinze Jr., Jason Biggs . . . the list goes on and on. The forefather of dark roots? Maybe. Distant cousin of ombré and dip-dye? Probably. Shorter-term impact than the decade's thin, overplucked eyebrows? For sure.

Frosted tips give off a fresh, vibrant, if a little bit punky, attitude, which is exactly the way you'll feel when you sip on this tonic-inflected Gin Rickey riff. Here, we dial back the gin a bit and substitute a pop of blanco tequila, which might seem like a careless choice, but trust me, it makes for one of the world's most unexpectedly amazing combos. Just don't forget to frost the tips of your mint with a dusting of sugar.

1 ounce gin
1 ounce blanco tequila
½ ounce fresh lime juice
½ ounce fresh lemon juice
3 ounces tonic water

GARNISH: MINT SPRIGS DUSTED WITH POWDERED SUGAR

 In a shaker, combine the gin, tequila, lime juice, and lemon juice. Fill with ice and shake vigorously for 15 seconds. Strain into a tall glass filled with ice. Top with the tonic water, garnish with a couple of mint sprigs dusted with sugar, and serve with a bubble tea straw.

Flag Code Punch

serves
4 to 6

From Hollister to Tommy Hilfiger, patriotic, flag-based clothing seemed to be everywhere in the '90s. The Old Navy Fourth of July T-shirt your parents made you wear really took on a subculture of its own—and, in fact, it's still going strong today. But a fun fact about clothes that feature the flag pattern is that they're all illegal. The US Flag Code states that: "No part of the flag should ever be used as a costume or athletic uniform." Oh well! Good thing there is no such thing as the flag police, otherwise we'd all be in a lot of trouble.

Fortunately, there is no rule against making red, white, and blue drinks. This one is fun for when you want to gather a few friends to celebrate summer (yay), this country (eh), or whatever else you want. The multicolored ice cubes may seem like a bit of a hassle, but they're easy to make and the visual wow factor more than makes up for the double freeze time. Just don't spill any on your flag shirt—*that* would be a violation.

24 ounces sparkling water, chilled
8 ounces blue curaçao
4 ounces bourbon
4 ounces Heart in a Blender Simple
   Syrup (page 141)

4 ounces fresh lemon juice
8 to 10 strawberry ice cubes (recipe
   follows)

In a large punch bowl, combine all the ingredients. Stir to mix well. Serve by ladling into old fashioned glasses.

Strawberry Ice Cubes

Makes 12 cubes

12 strawberries, tops trimmed
Whole milk
Filtered water, very chilled

Place the strawberries, flat side down, in an empty silicone ice cube tray, so that their tips are pointing up. Add a splash of milk to each. Transfer the tray to the freezer to let harden for at least 3 hours. Remove the tray from the freezer, fill each slot with water, and return to the freezer until completely frozen, at least another 3 hours. To use, remove the tray from the freezer and let thaw for 10 minutes at room temperature before gently popping out the cubes.

food
&
drink

SNACK PACK

Ultra-Cosmopolitan

makes 1 drink

The Cosmopolitan is basically synonymous with the '90s—but believe it or not, this classic cocktail was invented over the course of a few iterations at the tail end of the '80s. I guess that's true for a lot of us whose formative years took place in the '90s. The Cosmo rose to superstardom when it became the drink of choice for the ladies of *Sex and the City*. Legions of drinkers (mostly young straight women and gay men) ordered Cosmos night after night, eventually leading to an inevitable backlash among "craft" bartenders in later decades. Honestly, it took me a few years to accept this drink as a credible cocktail, which is also how I feel about Singapore Slings, Clover Clubs, and Strawberry Daiquiris—all "girly" drinks that have been unfairly maligned.

Just like we're better versions of ourselves twenty years later, so too is this Ultra-Cosmopolitan. It contains an elaborate grenadine syrup instead of simple straight cranberry juice to give the already-sophisticated cocktail another layer of accessories.

1½ ounces citron vodka
¾ ounce fresh lime juice
¾ ounce Ultragrenadine (page 71)
¾ ounce Cointreau or triple sec
GARNISH: LIME WHEEL

In a shaker, combine the drink ingredients. Add ice and shake vigorously for 15 seconds. Strain into a cocktail coupe. Garnish with the lime wheel on the rim of the glass.

1-800-FUN-COLOR

makes
1 drink

Do you remember a time when the blue M&M didn't exist? He (and his eyebrows) didn't come into the world until 1995. If you can't recall his origin story, let me refresh your memory: the Mars company wanted to replace the tan M&M with something a bit fresher and more youthful. So, as one does (perhaps more now than then), they set up an elaborate and expensive marketing campaign centered around public voting. People were encouraged to call 1-800-FUN-COLOR to choose pink, purple, or blue. I am pained to think that for a brief glimmer of time, the possibility of pink M&M's existed—I voted early and I voted often. I'm not a conspiracy theorist per se, but Mars never released a third-party audit of results, and I firmly believe the choice to pit pink against purple was a deliberate attempt to split the vote and assure blue's victory. (According to an AP report, more than 10 million votes were cast, of which blue won 54 percent—allegedly.)

What better way to indulge in a colorful conspiracy theory than with a cocktail that both looks and tastes like the blue M&M? Just be sure to use clear crème de cacao (it's labeled *white*). Without it, your drink will still taste good, but it won't have that blue hue that we've all now come to know and love . . . even though pink was robbed.

1½ ounces blanco tequila
1 ounce blue curaçao
¼ ounce white crème de cacao

 In a mixing glass or shaking tin, combine all the ingredients. Add ice and stir gently for 20 seconds. Strain into an old fashioned glass.

1-800- FUN COLOR

Gusher Crusher

One of my proudest achievements as a manipulative, too-smart-for-my-own-good child was convincing my mom that "fruit snacks" like Fruit by the Foot, Gushers, Fruit Roll-Ups, and Welch's Fruit Snacks were healthy. I would cannily scan the ingredients list for ammunition: "Look! They're mostly pear purée!" Somehow, that worked, though I sense parents these days might have caught on by now. I mostly exploited this loophole for Fruit by the Foot, wrapping it around my thumb and making it last for hours (which, in retrospect, is absolutely repulsive), but I really went wild for Gushers. I loved the almost-gross burst of sugar syrup inside the chewy shell. And do you want to know what's good in a very adult-looking drink? Gushers.

Here the Campari and raspberry liqueur offer a good amount of sweetness, but the key is to make sure the pick draws out the sweet, gooey Gushers nectar, dosing the drink with just the right hit of syrupy deliciousness. You might even convince your mom this is a classy drink.

1 ounce gin
1 ounce Kirschwasser
1 ounce raspberry liqueur
¾ ounce Campari
GARNISH: GUSHERS

In a mixing glass or small shaking tin, combine the drink ingredients. Add ice and stir gently for 20 seconds. Strain into a cocktail coupe. Garnish with four Gushers on a pick—and be sure their center goo is running straight into the drink.

The Devil's Food

One of the most pernicious bits of '90s marketing hype was this idea that we could eat whatever we wanted, as long as it was low-fat. Ice cream, yogurt, candy . . . these were all fine as long as there was little-to-no fat. One of the most iconic examples of this phenomenon was SnackWells cookies. Debuting in 1992, these treats were introduced as the answer to everyone's problems because they were cookies! But fat-free! What they didn't tell you is that they replaced all the fat with sugar, which made them even worse for you. (Do not even get me started on that other '90s diet "miracle," olestra.)

The vanilla cream sandwich cookies were just okay, but a confession: I thought, and still think, SnackWells Devil's Food cookies were legitimately good, and I am deeply sad they've been discontinued. This drink version of those dearly departed, definitely-not-good-for-you treats helps me drown my sorrows just a little bit.

1½ ounces Irish whiskey
1½ ounces heavy cream
½ ounce Heart in a Blender Simple Syrup (page 141)
½ ounce crème de cacao
2 dashes Angostura bitters
GARNISH: COCOA POWDER

 In a mixing glass or shaking tin, combine the drink ingredients. Add ice and stir gently for 20 seconds. Strain into a cocktail coupe. Dust cocoa powder over the top before serving.

Aaron BRRRR's Got Milk

"Got Milk?" ads took the world by storm in the '90s—but I have to ask the question: was it seriously such a big deal that people weren't drinking milk? The long-running campaign did an excellent job convincing Americans that the stuff was essential to our survival. The goopy milk-mustache print spots were no match for the TV commercials, my favorite of which was the one where the world's foremost Aaron Burr expert is prevented from winning a radio call-in contest by a too-dry peanut butter sandwich impeding his speech. If he'd had milk to wash it all down, he'd have closed the deal. Obviously, it won like every ad industry award in existence.

When you think about it, milk is kind of gross. It's . . . cow juice. But as a culinary tool, it's amazing; it has a combination of fat and protein that makes it excellent for all kinds of dishes and drinks. It's a key element in a White Russian, providing a rich base for the vodka and Kahlúa. This super frosty version may give you brain freeze, but no doubt it will pair perfectly with any PB&J.

4 cups ice
4 ounces whole milk
3 ounces Kahlúa
3 ounces vodka
¾ ounce Heart in a Blender Simple Syrup (page 141)
GARNISH: FRESH NUTMEG

In a blender, combine the drink ingredients. Blend on high until smooth, about 30 seconds. Divide the drink between two old fashioned glasses. Grate the nutmeg over the top of each before serving.

For You (and Them!)

Before beepers and then Nokia cell phones, the ultimate magic trick was pulling a roll of Hubba Bubba Bubble Tape out of your cargo shorts—it was the original pocket-based status symbol. The snarky earworm catchphrase: "Six feet of bubble gum, for you! Not them!" was far more enduring than the twenty-seven seconds it took for the gum to lose its flavor. The classic "bubble gum" flavor is actually a synthesis of common fruit flavors like strawberry, banana, and cherry, balanced by hints of cinnamon and mint. It's kind of like how white light is made up of all the colors in the rainbow.

Here we re-create this flavor in a large-format drink that, like the rope of gum itself, should give you plenty to share. With a drink this sweet, definitely make sure you're using the right amount of ice; you'll need to rely on its chill and dilution to balance out the sugar. It's a bubble gum drink—what do you expect?! Just make sure you savor it for longer than twenty-seven seconds.

4 ounces Cowabunga Sauce (page 84)
4 ounces banana liqueur
4 ounces Cherry Heering
1 ounce crème de menthe
½ ounce allspice liqueur
8 ounces Sprite, chilled

GARNISHES: FRESH SLICED STRAWBERRIES AND/OR KIWIS

In a punch bowl, combine the drink ingredients. Add 5 cups of ice, preferably crushed or pebble, if available. Stir briefly just to combine. Drop the strawberries and/or kiwis into the bowl to garnish. Serve with extra-long straws, forcing people to drink out of the bowl directly.

Yabba Dabba Doo

I don't know what was so fun about pushing mediocre sherbet through a paper towel tube, but cardboard-encased Flintstones Push-Up pops were simply some of the best supermarket desserts humanity has ever created. I had a beat-up Big Wheel tricycle that had handlebars that held the stick perfectly—it was like a dashboard iPhone holder, ages before its time. I used to ride around with my pop thinking I had everything figured out—which, obviously, I did.

When we turn this legendary frozen treat into a cocktail, what follows is a reasonably straightforward orange ice cream recipe with the addition of a French brandy–based orange liqueur. Perhaps there is some irony to the fact that in order to make this Stone-Age drink you need an ice cream machine, but it's worth the trouble. Because alcohol has a lower freezing point than water, you'll end up with a slightly liquid-y consistency, somewhere in the midpoint between ice cream and a slushie. Pretty much just like the texture of your pop after a few laps with the bike.

2 cups whole milk
1 cup granulated sugar
1½ tablespoons orange zest
2 cups fresh orange juice
½ ounce fresh lemon juice

¼ teaspoon kosher salt
1 vanilla bean, seeds scraped, or 2
   teaspoons pure vanilla extract
½ cup Grand Marnier, chilled

In a food processor or blender, combine the whole milk, sugar, orange zest, orange juice, lemon juice, salt, and vanilla seeds and process until the sugar is completely dissolved, about 45 seconds. Transfer to an airtight container and chill in the refrigerator for at least 3 hours or up to 12 hours.

Churn the mixture in ice cream machine according to manufacturer's instructions. Once nearly solid, pour in the Grand Marnier and churn until solid, about 5 more minutes. Serve immediately in a tall glass with a bubble tea straw and spoon. Store in an airtight container in the freezer for up to 2 weeks.

Dunkaroos Alexander

Was there anything cooler than busting out a packet of Dunkaroos in the middle school cafeteria? The answer is no. These portable little snack packs felt like the ultimate in both convenience and efficiency. You could have vanilla cookies and chocolate frosting whenever the mood struck you, which, if you were anything like me, was at 9:00 a.m. in geometry class.

A Brandy Alexander is an old classic cocktail featuring cream, crème de cacao, and brandy. It's a bit rich for modern palates, but there is a time and a place for almost every type of drink. What better way to revisit the sugar-soaked heyday of school lunches than by mixing up a Dunkaroos-infused cocktail? Here we make a few swaps to the classic Alexander recipe, notably adding vermouth and cold brew coffee. The creaminess comes, of course, from chocolate frosting, and even the cookies get to have a little fun dusting the rim of the glass. Mix up a couple of these to help you deal with your disillusion when you realize that Dunkaroos do not, in fact, come from Australia . . . and weren't even available there until 2019.

1 packet of Dunkaroos vanilla cookies with chocolate frosting
2 ounces rye whiskey
1 ounce cold brew coffee concentrate
1 ounce sweet vermouth
¼ ounce Heart in a Blender Simple Syrup (recipe opposite)

 On a plate, crush the Dunkaroos cookies into a fine powder. Using your finger, apply a rim of frosting around a cocktail coupe. Dip the frosted glass in the cookie powder to coat.

In a shaker, combine the whiskey, cold brew concentrate, vermouth, simple syrup, and the remaining chocolate frosting. Shake without ice for 5 seconds to incorporate the frosting, then fill with ice and shake vigorously for 15 seconds. Strain into the prepared glass.

Heart in a Blender Simple Syrup

Makes about 1½ cups

1 cup filtered water
1 cup granulated sugar

Combine the water and sugar in a blender. Blend on high until the sugar is completely dissolved, about 2 minutes. (Alternatively, and more traditionally, you can combine the water and sugar in a small saucepan over medium heat and cook, stirring until dissolved, about 1 minute. Let cool before using.)

Regardless of method, store the simple syrup in an airtight container in the refrigerator for up to 3 weeks or in the freezer for up to 3 months.

Parmesan Salt

Makes about ¼ cup

¼ cup freshly grated Parmesan cheese
2 tablespoons kosher salt

In a small bowl, combine the Parmesan and salt. Using the tips of your fingers, smoosh the salt and cheese together until evenly mixed. (Alternatively, you can use a spice grinder or mortar and pestle, if available.)

Pizza Anytime

Bagel Bites were peak convenience novelty food that rose to popularity in an era when parents were expected to—and wanted to—work regardless of their gender, and single-parent households were becoming increasingly acceptable and common. A whole generation of latchkey kids had to fend for themselves, home alone, until their parents got home from work to feed them properly. You'd have thought from the ad campaign—that still jingles in my head, and probably yours, too, to this day—that 24/7 availability of pizza was a critical societal issue that could only be solved by fusing the idea of pizza with breaded rounds that somewhat resembled bagels. Frozen, prepackaged, foolproof, solving a made-up crisis, and suspiciously fat-free . . . there was no way they weren't going to dominate.

This pizza bagel/Bloody Mary riff is a little bit more hands-on than its inspiration. The key is the flash infusion of everything bagel spice into the vodka to give you just the right amount of garlicky, sesame-y, poppy-seedy bite but without overdoing it. The Parmesan Salt rim is really fun, and you can use the leftovers for other food-based applications like salads and pasta so that, yeah, you can kinda have pizza anytime.

1 tablespoon everything bagel
    spice mix, plus more for garnish
2 ounces vodka
4 ounces marinara sauce
¾ ounce fresh lemon juice

⅛ teaspoon hot sauce
1 lemon wedge
Parmesan Salt (recipe opposite)
GARNISHES: PEPPERONI SLICE AND
    LEMON WEDGE

In a glass or small bowl, combine the everything bagel spice and the vodka. Let sit for 10 minutes to infuse, then strain the vodka through a fine-mesh strainer into a shaker, discarding the solids.

Add the marinara sauce, lemon juice, and hot sauce. Shake briefly, without ice, to combine.

Use a lemon wedge to moisten the rim of a tall glass and then dip it in the Parmesan Salt to coat the rim. Fill the glass with ice and pour in the contents of the shaker. Garnish with a pepperoni slice and a lemon wedge on a pick and sprinkle some everything bagel seasoning over the top. Serve with a bubble tea straw.

CapriRum

For such an unassuming, pouch-based lunchbox beverage, CapriSun has a pretty wild backstory. It was created in Germany in the 1960s under the brand name Capri Sonne. The drink was named after the popular Italian vacation destination Capri (*booyah!*), but by the time it hit its US stride in the '90s, its flavor roster was associated with pretty much any island and/or ocean. My favorite has always been the Tropical Punch, with Pacific Cooler in close second.

Now, you could always buy CapriSun and spike it with your favorite spirit, but it's way more fun to make your own with fruit liqueurs and fresh juices. Besides, then you don't have to worry about the environmental impact of all that foil, what to do when the straw falls off and gets lost, or, if you *can* find it, how to capably poke it into the pouch.

1½ ounces white rum
1 ounce banana liqueur
1 ounce blackberry liqueur
1 ounce pineapple juice, preferably fresh
1 ounce fresh lime juice
½ ounce Ultragrenadine (page 71)
GARNISHES: LUXARDO CHERRY AND PINEAPPLE WEDGE

 In a shaker, combine the drink ingredients. Add ice and shake vigorously for 15 seconds. Strain into a tall glass filled with ice. Garnish with a Luxardo cherry and pineapple wedge on a pick.

Fruity Scotch

Makes about 6 ounces

6 ounces blended Scotch whisky
⅓ cup sweet-and-fruity cereal, such as Fruity Pebbles

In a small bowl, combine the Scotch and cereal. Let sit for 30 minutes at room temperature, then strain the liquid through a fine-mesh strainer into an airtight container, discarding the cereal. Store in a cool, dry place for up to 1 month.

Balanced Breakfast

Cereal in the '90s had its very own spot on the food pyramid. Seemingly every few weeks, a new, somewhat absurd cereal would hit the market, causing kids (me) to beg their parents for trips to the grocery store. Some of these have endured—like Berry Berry Kix, Oreo O's, French Toast Crunch, Reese's Puffs, and Rice Krispies Treats cereal, to name a few—but forgotten classics include Yummy Mummy, Smurf-Berry Crunch, and C-3PO's. I was almost always denied satisfying this craving, but plenty of people seemed okay with the near-toxic levels of sugar as long as the cereal had 100 percent of your daily recommended amount of riboflavin. Part of a balanced breakfast! And obviously the best part of any and every sleepover with the lucky kids who had Cool Parents.

Integrating candy-like cereal into a cocktail can go two ways: double down on the inherent gustatory ghoulishness and make an overly sweet confection, or class up the cereal into something a bit more respectable. Much like my ~~fun~~ sugar-denying parents, I've taken this drink in the latter direction. Malty-rich Scotch is surprisingly compatible with a malty, fruity cereal like Fruity Pebbles; supporting this pairing are decadent Grand Marnier, sweet vermouth, and a touch of bone dry—but fruity—Kirschwasser. Fruity Pebbles are my personal starting point, but feel free to use any hyper-fruity cereal such as Froot Loops, Trix, or whatever you have in your pantry. Now that you're an adult, you can buy all the sugary cereal you want.

2 ounces Fruity Scotch (recipe opposite)
1 ounce sweet vermouth
½ ounce Kirschwasser
½ ounce Grand Marnier
GARNISH: ORANGE WEDGE

In a mixing glass or shaking tin, combine the drink ingredients. Add ice and stir gently for 20 seconds. Strain into an old fashioned glass filled with ice. Garnish with the orange wedge.

music

NOW THAT'S WHAT I CALL ...

Ray of Light

Madonna's career spans nearly four decades, but she really owned the '90s. She entered the decade hot off her Blond Ambition world tour and exited as one of the most powerful figures in pop music. Her 1998 album, *Ray of Light*, was peak genre-hopping Madonna. She teamed up with music producer William Orbit to create an album that mixed and matched various styles and influences. It also represented an evolution of her vocal performance following her training to prepare for her role in *Evita*.

Like the album, this bright, bubbly cocktail is a mash-up of a few different influences: you can see traces of classic cocktails like the Corpse Reviver No. 2, Margarita, and French 75. It will make you feel like you just got home.

1½ ounces blanco tequila
¾ ounce fresh lemon juice
½ ounce yellow Chartreuse
½ ounce Turbo Honey Syrup (page 63)
3 ounces sparkling wine

 In a shaking tin, combine the tequila, lemon juice, yellow Chartreuse, and honey syrup. Add ice and shake vigorously for 15 seconds. Strain into a large cocktail coupe. Top with the sparkling wine.

Dookie

Green Day's Grammy Award–winning 1994 album *Dookie* was on heavy
rotation on my cassette radio. Squeezed in between En Vogue and Ace of
Base, the pop-punk-grunge aesthetic and nihilistic lyrics had me hooked in a
different way, even though it took me a few years to realize what "Longview"
was really about.

Despite the name of the album suggesting . . . what it suggests . . . here we
still have a sludgy, vaguely green-brown drink that's equal parts weird and
appetizing. The key is to purée pineapple and freeze it into chunks and put
them to double duty: first, they act as shaking ice, chilling and diluting the
drink. Then, as they melt, the drink gets sweeter, softer, and chunkier. What
more could you want from a drink named Dookie?

2 cups roughly chopped fresh pineapple
1½ ounces green Chartreuse
½ ounce reposado tequila
2 ounces ginger ale, chilled

In a blender or food processor, purée the pineapple until smooth,
about 30 seconds. Pour the mixture into a silicone ice cube tray and
let freeze overnight. Remove from the freezer about 10 minutes
before using.

In a shaker, combine the green Chartreuse, tequila, and 3 to 5
pineapple cubes. Shake vigorously for 15 seconds. Pour the entire
contents of the shaker into a wine glass and top with the ginger ale.
Serve immediately.

Boy Band Vaporware

serves
4

The '90s were the era of peak boy band. A lot of the Disney TV stars came of age during this decade, and their natural progression was from Saturday morning shows to full-fledged pop stars with legions of adoring fans and borderline inappropriately horny videos. *NSYNC, the Backstreet Boys, 98 Degrees, Hanson . . . these icons paved the way for some epic solo careers, but also for today's One Direction, BTS, and, yes, the Jonas Brothers. You'd be hard pressed to find a teenager without a *Tiger Beat* and/or *YM* tear-out of at least one of these boys on their bedroom wall. (I personally was a fan of both JC Chasez and Jeff Timmons.) Another phenomenon, coined in the '80s but made popular in the '90s, was "vaporware," software that was announced but never released. One of its most famous usages was in the United States' antitrust case against Microsoft in 1994.

In 2018, the Backstreet Boys made headlines when they announced they would be launching their own tequila. But that has so far proven to be liquid vaporware. That said, you can make this drink with any of the delicious tequilas already on the market. It's a batchable, light-but-boozy cocktail that, when frozen, takes on a little bit of texture. Either enjoy it as is, or let it sit out for 5 minutes if you want something smoother, like Nick Carter's voice.

6 ounces Fino sherry
4½ ounces reposado tequila
4½ ounces St-Germain
4½ ounces filtered water, chilled

In an airtight container, combine all the ingredients and stir to mix well. Chill in the refrigerator for at least 4 hours. When ready to serve, pour into cocktail coupes.

Note: This drink can be stored in the refrigerator for up to 2 weeks or in the freezer for up to 2 months. When serving from the freezer, allow the drink to sit at room temperature for 10 minutes before pouring.

Zombie

The Cranberries' 1994 hit single "Zombie" was played, I think, on average twenty times per hour on my local top-40 radio station, Z-100. Lead singer Dolores O'Riordan's vocals cried out against the violence in Northern Ireland, giving the song that precise blend of pop, rock, femme, antiwar activist vibe that we all gobbled up in the '90s.

The song was and is awesome on so many levels, one of which is that there is an equally awesome classic cocktail of the same name. The Zombie was invented by Donn Beach in the 1930s for his Don the Beachcomber chain of restaurants, and its recipe was a closely guarded secret for many years. Fortunately, we've had about a century to figure it out. This particular Zombie recipe is an approximation of the original, still served in the traditional tropical mug but slightly pared down in complexity. With a longer ingredient list, it's a challenging yet accessible piece of history.

1½ ounces dark rum
1½ ounces overproof Jamaican rum
¾ ounce fresh lime juice
¾ ounce fresh grapefruit juice
½ ounce Ultragrenadine (page 71)
¼ ounce absinthe
2 dashes Angostura bitters
GARNISH: MINT SPRIG

 In a shaker, combine the drink ingredients. Add ice and shake vigorously for 15 seconds. Strain into a tropical mug. Garnish with the mint sprig and serve with a straw.

Ziggazig-ah

Like the United States, the UK is a mixed bag of good and bad, but the pop supergroup the Spice Girls, we can safely say, has left the world a better place. Despite being manufactured by a record label and sheathed with a surface-level feminist aesthetic, something was genuinely captivating about these five women and their glittery "girl power" message, especially before such messaging was over-commoditized. Each of us found a little bit of ourselves in at least one member of the group.

Cramming the entire essence of the Spice Girls into one drink would be tricky, as they indeed hit many, many notes. But this "spiced" riff on the classic Southside cocktail uses gin, ginger (obviously), black pepper, and cucumber to serve up a decidedly British vibe that'll speak to you whether you identified as Sporty, Scary, Baby, Ginger, or Posh—or some combination thereof.

1½ ounces gin
¾ ounce fresh lime juice
½ ounce Ginger Syrup (page 54)
¼ ounce Heart in a Blender Simple Syrup (page 141)
3 slices English cucumber
3 cranks freshly ground black pepper
GARNISHES: SLICED CUCUMBER AND GINGER CANDY

In a shaker, combine the drink ingredients. Muddle to break up the cucumber, then add ice. Shake vigorously for 15 seconds and fine strain into a cocktail coupe (see Note below). Garnish with the cucumber slice and ginger candy on a pick.

Note: To fine strain, hold a small fine-mesh strainer underneath the shaker as you pour the drink into the glass. This extra step filters out any tiny solid bits that you don't want to get stuck in your teeth.

Waterfall Chaser

TLC's music was in heavy rotation for me, and probably for you, too. I think "No Scrubs" might have been their most popular track, but "Waterfalls" was also one of their biggest hits—and the CGI effects in the video were, at the time, mind-blowing. Like a lot of the music I listened to in the '90s, the safe sex–PSA-inflected lyrics were totally lost on me. I just liked the song.

TLC exemplified effortless cool and classy ferocity, and this sangria recipe encapsulates that exact vibe. Sangrias are in a class of drinks that require patience: if you put all of these ingredients together and drink immediately, you'll be disappointed by the results. As "Waterfalls" advises, it's best to not go too fast; let the fruit soak at least overnight. If you have the patience, this mixture improves day over day, for up to two weeks—if you can wait that long.

2 cups finely chopped cantaloupe
2 small oranges, finely chopped
1 lemon, finely chopped
1 (750-mL) bottle medium-dry white wine, such as sauvignon blanc
4 ounces St-Germain
4 ounces Cognac
8 ounces sparkling water
GARNISH: SAGE LEAVES

In a large airtight container, combine the cantaloupe, oranges, lemon, wine, St-Germain, and Cognac. Stir for 5 seconds, cover, and refrigerate for at least 8 hours, preferably overnight, and up to 2 weeks. When ready to serve, transfer the mixture to a large pitcher and add the sparkling water. Pour into wine glasses and garnish each with the sage leaves.

Barbie Girl

I must have listened to Danish pop group Aqua's 1997 hit single "Barbie Girl" hundreds of times. Even just hearing the first line, "I'm a Barbie Girl," it immediately gets stuck in your head (sorry about that). Despite never having played with Barbies, I loved the vaguely techno, Europop sound and somewhat saucy lyrics. Mattel, makers of the actual Barbie dolls, were not so pleased. They sued the group's record label, MCA, for violating their trademark and tarnishing the toy's long-standing wholesome reputation. A countersuit followed, and both cases were ultimately dismissed with the presiding judge issuing this iconic line: "The parties are advised to chill." Has anything ever been more '90s?

This song, and this anecdote, lives in a glossy, syrupy-slick world that sounds like a blast to visit. This combination of fresh watermelon juice, vibrant grape brandy, and black currant liqueur will take you there immediately. Come on, Barbie, let's go party.

2 ounces fresh watermelon juice
1½ ounces pisco
¾ ounce crème de cassis
½ ounce fresh lime juice
GARNISH: LUXARDO CHERRIES

 In a shaker, combine the drink ingredients. Fill with ice and shake vigorously for 15 seconds. Strain into a cocktail coupe. Garnish with Luxardo cherries on a pick.

Tejano Michelada

makes
1 drink

Despite her tragically short life, Selena Quintanilla had a profound effect on American music. She helped to popularize Tejano music, a uniquely Mexican style that hybridizes Mexican-Spanish vocals with German and Czech influences like waltz and polka. Selena's 1994 album, *Amor Prohibito*, was the first Tejano album to hit platinum status and remains the bestselling Tejano album of all time today.

This Michelada riff celebrates the tremendous achievement and the impact Selena has made overall. It relies on a German (or Czech)-style beer and avocado-infused tequila. The avocado infusion is a standard fat wash technique in which alcohol is used to lift flavor from fat, and the result is a round richness without any greasiness.

1 pint Pilsner beer
1 ounce Avo-quila (recipe follows)
1 ounce fresh lime juice
½ ounce hot sauce, preferably Cholula
GARNISHES: KOSHER SALT AND FRESHLY GROUND BLACK PEPPER

In a large pint glass, combine the drink ingredients. Stir gently to combine. Just before serving, sprinkle salt and pepper over the top of the drink.

Avo-quila

Makes about 12 ounces

12 ounces reposado tequila
½ medium avocado, finely chopped

In an airtight container, combine the tequila and avocado and stir to combine. Refrigerate for at least 8 hours, preferably overnight. Strain through a fine-mesh strainer. Store in the refrigerator for up to 2 weeks.

Sky's the Limit

Tupac Shakur's death in 1996 and the Notorious B.I.G.'s in 1997 were the culmination of a longtime East Coast versus West Coast feud. These two deaths had a deep impact on not only the rap industry, but also on our culture at large. The music video that accompanies Biggie's posthumously released song "Sky's the Limit" is truly a sight to behold. Director Spike Jonze, a '90s legend in his own right, created the most perfect, bittersweet tribute to the slain rapper. The video features teenagers playacting a traditional '90s mansion-and-luxury-cars hip-hop video; it's equal parts memento mori and send-up. In the last moments, the kids are sitting around the table in a lavish restaurant drinking what can only be described as mocktails—most likely Shirley Temples.

When *I* was a child in the '90s, getting to order a Shirley Temple was the height of fanciness when my family went out to dinner. This straightforward rendition is augmented by an elaborate "ultra" grenadine made from saffron, black tea, cranberry juice, and pomegranate juice, which makes it luxury for all ages. No pun intended, but this drink is very spike-able, if you are so inclined. Try tossing in one or two ounces of gin, vodka, or Cognac.

7 ounces ginger ale
1 ounce Ultragrenadine (page 71)
GARNISHES: LUXARDO CHERRIES AND GINGER CANDY

Fill a wine glass with ice. Add the drink ingredients and stir briefly. Garnish with the Luxardo cherries and ginger candy on a pick.

Salt-N-Pepa Lemonade

I have been an evangelist for black pepper in drinks for most of my career. Sure, black pepper might feel like a basic spice given its ubiquity on dinner tables, but the good stuff, freshly ground, can transform a beverage—especially a nonalcoholic one like this.

Speaking of ubiquity, thanks to smash singles like "Shoop" and "Whatta Man," hip-hop group Salt-N-Pepa was inescapable in the '90s. Sure, a substantial portion of their lyrics went over my head—and probably yours, too—but this drink makes up for lost time. Seasoning a sugar syrup with salt-n-pepa might seem like an unorthodox choice, but this salty-sweet-spicy blend is as bright as the sun (and I wanna have some fun). Feel free to add some vodka or tequila if you want to turn the volume up to 10.

3 ounces filtered water or sparkling water, chilled
1½ ounces fresh lemon juice
1½ ounces Salt-N-Pepa Syrup (recipe follows)
GARNISH: MINT SPRIG

 In a shaker, combine the drink ingredients. Add ice and shake vigorously for 15 seconds. Strain into a tall glass filled with ice. Garnish with the mint sprig.

Salt-N-Pepa Syrup
Makes about 1 cup

1 cup Heart in a Blender Simple Syrup (page 141)
Zest of 4 lemons
½ teaspoon fine sea salt
¾ teaspoon freshly ground black pepper

In a sealable container, combine all the ingredients. Let sit for 30 minutes. Strain the mixture through a fine-mesh strainer into an airtight container, discarding the solids. Store the syrup in the refrigerator for up to 3 weeks or in the freezer for up to 3 months.

Closer to God

makes 1 drink

Was it just me, or was Nine Inch Nails a bit intense for an early teen? I was vibing more on Janet Jackson and the Spin Doctors. But as I got a bit older, I learned to love the industrial, synthy, and, frankly, poppy sounds of musician Trent Reznor's band. The first album I bought of theirs was 1999's magnum opus *The Fragile*—but I'd bet that at a minimum, you're familiar with 1994's smash hit "Closer," and you probably loved the scandalous feeling you got from singing it aloud.

The lyrics of "Closer" comprise a nihilistic love (lust?) song about giving over your entire being to someone else. One way to do this—in liquid form—is via the nihilistic cocktail, the Mind Eraser. Despite being a drink that's recently joined the canon, its exact origins are impossible to determine. It shares a nihilistic vibe with '90s NIN because it's basically just a vehicle for vodka. By layering the Kahlúa beneath and sparkling water on top, and then pulling from the bottom with a straw when you drink it, the liqueur will hit first, coating the mouth, followed by the bracing and clearing vodka, followed up by the crisp cleansing bubbles. It hits hard, but it's over before you know it.

2 ounces Kahlúa
2 ounces vodka
3 ounces sparkling water

Fill a tall glass with ice. Gently pour the Kahlúa into the bottom of the glass. Once the Kahlúa has settled, gently pour the vodka over it. Finally, gently pour the sparkling water on the top of the drink. Serve with a long straw that reaches the base of the glass.

It's Oat So Quiet

Pop divas like Britney, Christina, and, of course, Madonna ruled the '90s, but Björk was my own esoteric Icelandic queen. She's best remembered for her iconic swan dress at the 2001 Oscars, but even before that I loved her singular mix of indie electronic beats set to a wild and kaleidoscopic vocal performance. She released "It's Oh So Quiet" in 1995 as a single; it's a cover of a German song from the late 1940s, but the Spike Jonze–directed video is what makes it. Comprised of various slo-mo and normal-speed scenes of Björk and a troupe of dancers prancing around an auto shop, the video ends with Björk floating above the crowd before issuing a final "shhhh" to the viewer.

This nonalcoholic blend of hot oat milk and chamomile-infused honey syrup is at least a start at achieving that sense of peace and quiet Björk was nudging us toward. The calming aromas, especially the nutmeg on top, would work perfectly to help you wind down after a wild night of prancing around anywhere.

8 ounces oat milk
1 ounce Turbo Honey Syrup (page 63)
GARNISH: FRESH NUTMEG

 In a heatproof mug, combine the drink ingredients and stir briefly to combine. Microwave on medium-high for 90 seconds. Grate generous amounts of nutmeg over the top.

In Bloom

One of the benefits and really purposes of having an older sibling is access to way cooler music than you deserved when you were growing up. Thanks to my brother (hi, Ned) I learned about grunge bands like Nirvana, Pearl Jam, and the Stone Temple Pilots. To me it was gritty and unfussy, while at the same time poppy, ironic, and even a bit pretty.

What could be more grunge than making a cocktail in a beer can? Let me tell you: nothing. In-can cocktails are great for places like concerts where you have limited access to the trappings of civilization like running water and glassware. Here, St-Germain lends sweetness and floral notes, while the aquavit affords a distinctly alternative caraway and star anise flavor. To get the maximum vibe here, use Krogstad, an aquavit producer based in Portland, Oregon, for an extra taste of the PNW.

1 (12-ounce) can light beer, chilled
1 ounce vodka
¾ ounce St-Germain
½ ounce aquavit

 Open the beer and drink or pour out 2 to 3 ounces (one big sip). Pour the vodka, St-Germain, and aquavit into the can and jiggle it around a bit to mix.

Gin-ey in a Bottle

For some reason, the '90s had us pitting Britney and Christina and Jessica and others against each other. It makes sense to a certain extent—they were trying to sell records after all—but the zero-sum narrative was the proto-version of today's wildly toxic stan culture. Now we know there's enough success for everyone to go around; loving one pop princess does not take away from any other, and we can all just share in our enjoyment of these amazing women.

While these ladies were all fabulous and made an enduring impression on the decade overall, I had a particular soft spot for Christina Aguilera's "Genie in a Bottle." In the spirit of sharing success, whip up this batchable and, perhaps most important, *pretty* gin potion for when your body's sayin' "let's go."

6 ounces gin
3 ounces dry vermouth
1½ ounces crème de cassis
1 ounce filtered water, chilled

In an airtight container, combine all the ingredients. Chill in the refrigerator for at least 4 hours. When ready to serve, pour into cocktail coupes.

Note: You can store the drink in the refrigerator for up to 2 weeks or in the freezer for up to 2 months. When serving from the freezer, allow the drink to sit at room temperature for 10 minutes before pouring.

Free Your Mind

At the tender age of ten years old, I played my cassette copy of En Vogue's *Funky Divas* hundreds of times. The lyrics to "Giving Him Something He Can Feel," "My Lovin' (You're Never Gonna Get It)," among others, are permanently seared into my memory. In 1992, I was too young (and definitely too white) to fully grasp the meaning of their hit single, "Free Your Mind." Even today, the song's forceful rejection of anti-Black racism, misogyny, and the pain of Black women still feels relevant, as there is still so much work to be done in the name of liberation for all.

Back then I was far too young to even think about mixing drinks, but if I could send a cocktail back in time to my fourth-grade self singing along to this album in my bedroom, this would be the one. Lapsang Souchong, a smoky black tea variant, offers a set of aromatics similar to what you might find in a smoky Scotch whisky, while Luxardo cherries provide a sophisticated sweetness. Tonic water is a great addition since it provides a sharp bitterness and acidity for balance.

1 tablespoon loose Lapsang Souchong tea leaves
2 tablespoons Luxardo cherries in syrup
3 ounces fresh watermelon juice
½ ounce fresh lemon juice
1½ ounces tonic water

In a shaker, combine the tea leaves and cherries and muddle to break up the cherries. Add the watermelon juice and lemon juice. Add ice and shake vigorously for 15 seconds. Fine strain into a cocktail coupe (see Note on page 159). Top with the tonic water to finish.

Caribbean Blue

If Enya's 1991 multiplatinum album *Shepherd Moons* wasn't in your parents' five-disc CD changer, were you even living? For some reason this album was one of the few things my WASPy parents, emo older brother, and my dweeby self could all agree on. The blissy, layered vocals did the trick when it came time to put something on at dinnertime.

Thanks to the unauthorized (but later okayed) sample by the Fugees for their hit "Ready or Not," "Boadicea" is likely the most famous of Enya's tracks, but "Caribbean Blue" is my personal favorite. It's kinda waltzy and mostly nonsensical, which also happens to be exactly how I like my drinks. Here, the infusion of coconut into blue curaçao is an entirely optional step, but it adds an appealing layer, transporting you away to a synthy, tropical paradise.

1 ounce pineapple juice, preferably fresh
¾ ounce vodka
¾ ounce white rum
¾ ounce Co-Curaçao (recipe follows)
¾ ounce fresh lime juice

GARNISHES: RESERVED BLUE COCONUT FLAKES (SEE BELOW) AND PINEAPPLE SLICE

 In a shaker, combine the drink ingredients. Fill with ice and shake vigorously for 15 seconds. Pour the entire contents of the shaker (including the ice) into an old fashioned glass. To garnish, press the pineapple slice into the dried blue coconut flakes and perch it on the rim of the glass.

Co-Curaçao
Makes about 3 ounces

4 ounces blue curaçao
2 tablespoons unsweetened shredded coconut

In a small bowl, combine the blue curaçao and coconut. Stir and let sit for 30 minutes. Strain the liquid through a fine-mesh strainer into an airtight container, reserving the coconut flakes. Spread out the soaked coconut flakes on a sheet pan and let dry for about 5 hours. Store the infused blue curaçao and the coconut flakes in separate airtight containers in a cool, dry place for up to 3 weeks.

Acknowledgments

To everyone directly responsible for this book:

Nicole Tourtelot, my amazing agent and constant counsel.

Amanda Englander, my editor who (again) made this book immeasurably better than I could have on my own.

My loving and lovely husband **Michael Remaley** who, in addition to my baseline hijinks, endured months of chaotic test kitchen vibes (and questionable drink prototypes).

My taste testing team of **Shoshana Goldberg, Noah Eisenkraft, Paul D'Avino,** and **Lux Alptraum** who braved a late winter night to make sure I was not totally off the rails.

Ian Dingman and **Clara Fitzpatrick,** your creativity brought this book to life.

The rest of the team at Union Square & Co.: **Caroline Hughes, Lindsay Herman, Chris Stambaugh, Marina Padakis Lowry, Kevin Iwano, Melissa Farris, Blanca Oliviery, Elke Villa, Emily Meehan.**

To my wider circle of emotional and material support:

Paul and Stefana deBary and my extended deBary family; Leslie and Charles Rousell; Joan and George Hellman; Julia Bainbridge; Youngmi Mayer and Alex Pemoulié, Kerrin Egalka; Ariane Hardjowirogo; Bex Palkovics and Mike Van Dorn; Hannah Coleman; Brette Warshaw; Jena Derman; Buzzy Cohen; Anna-Lisa Campos; Christina Turley; Karen Fu; Tori Preston;

Bob Harper; David Chang; Pamela Herron; Kelly Issac; Sam Fore; Shannon Mustipher; and **April Watchtel.**

To my mentors and early believers: **Jim Meehan, David Chang, Kate Krader, Robert Petrarca, Dave Arnold, David Wondrich, Julie Reiner, Brad Thomas Parsons,** and **Theresa Paopao.**

To **Tiffani Theissen:** I cannot begin to describe what a surreal honor it is to share space in this book with you.

To two most excellent books about the '90s, **Chuck Klosterman**'s *Nineties* and **Brian Raftery**'s *Best. Movie. Year. Ever.*, as well as YouTube, Tumblr, and the Instagram's algorithm, all for their assistance with my copious research.

And to the friends I made in the '90s who are still hanging with me: **Jonathan Rousell; Reid Wedding, Charlie Taney, Will Crowley, Ryan Mullally, Leland Benton; Nikki Allen, Katie Regan; Matt Bernstein; Shiri Sandler; Amanda Dolan; Zuki Tanaka.** My memories of that decade are deeply intertwined with your presence and make every moment shine with vivid warmth.

And, finally, to my late mother, **Victoria deBary,** whose voice I will never get out of my head.

Index

Index

UNION
SQUARE
& CO.
NEW YORK

UNION SQUARE & CO. and the distinctive Union Square & Co. logo are trademarks of Sterling Publishing Co., Inc.

Union Square & Co., LLC, is a subsidiary of Sterling Publishing Co., Inc.

ISBN 978-1-4549-4708-0
ISBN 978-1-4549-4709-7 (e-book)

For information about custom editions, special sales, and premium purchases, please contact specialsales@unionsquareandco.com.

Printed in China

10 9 8 7 6 5 4 3 2 1

unionsquareandco.com

Illustrator: Clara Kirkpatrick
Editor: Amanda Englander
Editorial assistant: Caroline Hughes
Designer: Ian Dingman
Production editor: Lindsay Herman
Copy editor: Terry Deal
Production manager: Kevin Iwano
Indexer: Jay Kreider